THE GANGSTER FILM

by John Baxter

$3·50   *Above : Chicago Confidential*   21s. £1.05

The
GANGSTER FILM
by JOHN BAXTER

A. ZWEMMER LTD, LONDON
A.S. BARNES & CO., NEW YORK

Acknowledgments

MY thanks to the following people who supplied information: Richard Brennan; Ian Klava; Chris Collier; Charles Higham; and David Stratton. For stills I am indebted to Joan Saint; Richard Brennan; Bob Vogel of Metro-Goldwyn-Mayer (New York); Kevin Smith of the House of Dare, Sydney; Charles Gilbert and Ray Edmondson of the National Library, Film Division, Canberra, for access to the Taussig collection; John Downs of Universal Pictures, Sydney; Warner Brothers/ Seven Arts, Sydney; Jim Sayle of Paramount Pictures, Sydney; Tony Malone of Columbia Pictures, Sydney; and Barrie Pattison.

Primary references for the factual sections of the book were *The Bootleggers* (Kenneth Allsop), *The Dillinger Days* (John Toland), *Persons in Hiding* (J. Edgar Hoover) and the files of the New York *Times,* for access to which I am grateful to the Public Library of New South Wales, Sydney.

Useful guidelines for my approach to this book were given by Richard Whitehall's "Crime Inc." (*Films and Filming,* January, February and March, 1964.)

COVER STILLS
Front: Warren Beatty and Faye Dunaway in Penn's *Bonnie and Clyde*
(courtesy of Warner-Pathe)
Back: James Cagney and Humphrey Bogart in Walsh's *The Roaring Twenties*

Preface

THE gangster film is not an easy area of the cinema about which to write. One does not have the flexible yardstick of setting on which to rely; although most films set in the American West between 1830 and 1910 can reasonably be classed as Westerns, it would be idle to claim that any urban crime melodrama set between 1920 and the present is a gangster film. In its pure form, in fact, the gangster film existed only for a few years in America during the Thirties, when it reflected the national preoccupation with the breakdown in law and order. Since that time it has spread so much that the coherence it once had has disappeared. We no longer find it odd to see Richard Widmark's performance in the Western *Yellow Sky* related to his gangster image, nor to see a story of juvenile delinquency set to music as *West Side Story*.

No reader is likely to agree totally with the films I have selected to list in this book. Purists will claim, with justice, that I have exceeded my brief by including films that relate only in the most general way to organised crime—"private eye" dramas, for instance, and stories of detection like *Panic in the Streets*. Others, searching in vain for a murder mystery or thriller on which they need information, will argue that a book which includes Siodmak's *The Killers* should surely include the same director's *Phantom Lady*. Perhaps. I can only plead that a book containing every crime drama ever filmed would be enormous, one that listed only the "pure" gangster films tiny.

My compromise has been to list films that deal, even in a general way, with *organised* as opposed to conventional crime. This I have bent to cover plots to kill or rob, even if the group involved is small, but stories of individual theft or killing have, as a general rule, been excluded. On the other hand, one only has to recall that "classic" gangster films like *The Maltese Falcon* and *The Big Sleep* contain few, if any, elements of organised crime to see that this rule was made to be broken.

In an effort to cover more ground and, more importantly, to relate the gangster films to the period that produced them, a vital step in understanding them, I have included a number of longer entries on types of gangster film and on individuals who have become popular subjects for film biographies. Again, I may disappoint those who are looking for material on Homer Van Meter, "Baby Face" Nelson or "Mad Dog" Coll, all excluded by my rule of thumb to include only those who had at least two films made about them.

No book of film reference is perfect, and this, due to the subject's diffusion, less than most. But I hope that the readership for which it is intended, the filmgoer who seeks readily accessible information on the subject, cast and crew of a film, usually to decide whether it is worth watching on television, finds it a useful tool.

James Cagney in 13 RUE MADELEINE

Introduction

"ORDINARY people of your class," the killer Dancer says contemptuously in Don Siegel's *The Line Up*, "You don't understand the criminal's need for violence." The remark is typical of the modern gangster film. Like them, it implies that the rules of crime are different from those of ordinary society, and force on those who live by them a unique and rigorous ethic. "Crime is only a left-handed form of human endeavour," Louis Calhern says in *The Asphalt Jungle,* conveying in one sentence the code of these haunted people.

Characteristic too is the way in which Dancer's comment hints at social generalisation. It is not only the criminal commenting on other criminals; it is the criminal commenting on society, and the forces that encouraged him to enter the half-world of crime. Few gangster films are free of the imputation that criminals are the creation of society rather than rebels against it. It is because this was often in the past true, and may still be, that the gangster film has become the province of men whose political and social views are unconventional.

Our ambiguous attitude to criminals, figures both of menace and glamour, has formed the basic gangster film character, the urban wolf. He is the product of his harsh environment, violent, laconic and tough, but his involvement in crime seems a matter of chance rather than choice. An urban wolf can equally well be killer or detective, warden or prisoner. The ethics are similar, and all speak the same discursive language. When early gangster films took as their theme the conflict between boyhood friends who end up on opposite sides of the law, the writers, although always giving equal time to statements from both sides on the desirability of the alternatives, were usually forced by the subtlety of the distinction to settle the matter by violence.

True to the traditions of the entertainment film, the urban wolves, like Western heroes and the characters of science fiction and fantasy films, have strict and limited dimensions. They are almost always men in early middle-age; only they have had the chance to live, and to cultivate the strict moral code which justifies their existence. (The real gangsters were usually young—Al Capone's golden period ended in 1929, when he was thirty-four—but the cinema has never been sensitive to the truth in recording reality, as the sections in this book on real criminals and their screen incarnations show.)

A certain ironic humour and mordant philosophy are also common to both gangster and cop, each seeming able to express himself with wit and perception about his relative role in a way real men would find ludicrous. And they are united in their contempt for the amateur, the unprofessional, the "punks" interested only in profit, the "freaks" who kill for fun or terrorise without point. In *The Asphalt Jungle* this coincidence of attitude is intelligently underlined. Cop John McIntire early in the film orders his men to squeeze a witness of information by locking him up, frightening him some more. "Don't you know your job?" he snaps. And later, in an identical mood, gunman Sterling Hayden beats up a man who has tried to double-cross him, and snarls, "What kinda guy are you anyhow? Try to shake us down and don't have the guts to go through with it." For both, the rituals of professionalism seem more important than the formal necessities of crime and detection.

It is idle to generalise too much about gangster films, or any other field of cinema, so immense are the variations, particularly in Hollywood where most *genres* have been crossed successfully. Gangsters have appeared in comedies, musicals, horror and science fiction films, Shakespeare has been done as a gangster film, and there have been films about dogs reincarnated as private eyes and hardened killers moved to repent after hearing Billy Graham. But in general the best have been tied closely to the reality of crime, reflecting public interest in a particular criminal, robbery or illegal activity. The history of the gangster film is in a sense the history of crime in the United States, and few of the best films have not taken some of their material from the reality of organised crime which is a part of modern urban life.

* * *

Crime in America is an imported vice. No doubt it would have existed had the first waves of migration in the late Nineteenth century not brought to the United States many of the underworld elements of European cities, but it would have been a lesser kind of crime, neither so ferocious nor so well-organised as it was to become. With the migrants came representatives of the tightly organised street gangs of French and Italian cities, the violent political activists of Ireland and the Balkans, the blood-loyal *mafiosi* of Sicily. The influx laid the foundations of the fanatical and brutal criminal society of the Twenties. As Kenneth Allsop points out, "the gangster of the Prohibition era was almost invariably second-generation American; he was almost invariably a Sicilian, an Irishman or a Jew." It was mainly from the sons of the 1880s' immigrants that the underworld drew its most apt recruits.

Although the Mafia was in New York in the 1890s, its activities were limited by the meagre sources of revenue. D. W. Griffith in *The Musketeers of Pig Alley* (1912) showed how the street gangs of the time existed, ruling a few blocks, getting along on the proceeds of extortion and petty theft, a far cry from the profitable and well-organised activity of Italy, where in many communities the Mafia and local government were often indistinguishable. But the tempo of criminal life quickened in the period following the First World War, when soldiers, demobbed to unemployment, social unrest and injustice, turned to civil disobedience, union agitation and sometimes crime as a means of satisfying their taste for violence and their need for the necessities of life.

Into this potentially explosive situation the United States government in 1920 introduced prohibition of liquor, the nation's most disastrous social experiment. The European gangs found themselves with the ingredients of an illegal industry, bootlegging. Fattened by a rising market, already dissatisfied with a lax and cynical government, the public was not inclined to obey a puritan injunction to abstain, and welcomed as social institutions the illegal liquor merchant and secret bar. From among the unemployed ex-soldiers, the gangs drew men who had little respect for a government that had denied them social justice, a work force at once eager to advance and careless of whom they hurt in doing so. All over the United States, but particularly in Chicago where geographical and social conditions favoured the illegal liquor industry, the gangs fastened onto this new source of revenue and used it greedily to establish themselves.

* * *

Evelyn Brent and Clive Brook in PARTNERS IN CRIME

With Prohibition, the legends of crime began. By the middle Twenties, the public was becoming aware of certain individuals in the underworld who carried off their careers with flair, arrogance and a style unusual in the characteristically anonymous world of crime. One was Arnold Rothstein, New York bootlegger, gambler and racketeer, the original of Meyer Wolfsheim in F. Scott Fitzgerald's *The Great Gatsby,* Nathan Detroit in Damon Runyon's *Guys and Dolls* sketches, as well as of films like *Street of Chance* (1930), *The Big Bankroll* (1959) and a score of others. The stereotype of the brightly dressed, clever and arrogant gang boss is derived directly from him.

The second figure who emerged as big news was Al Capone, the boy from Castel Amaro who, before he was thirty, had taken over Chicago and the national boot-legging industry. Public interest in Capone, Rothstein and people like them led to a string of autobiographical films, many based on actual figures. Most sought only to tell the story of a gangster's rise and fall, and were usually riotously amoral and violent until the last reel when, as a sop to the pious, he was shown shot down by the law. Ben Hecht's observation, that "the forces of law and order did not advance on the villains with drawn guns but with their palms out like bellboys," was seldom observed in these phony fantasies of violence and sado-eroticism.

Rothstein was killed in 1928 and Capone jailed in 1931, but they left behind a legacy that would rack America for decades, and also provide Hollywood with the basis for its next cycle of crime films. Both men had realised that profit depended on organisation and co-operation between gangs. Rothstein in New York and Capone in Chicago had put order above all, welding the dissident gangs into efficient mobs even if mass extermination was the only means whereby this could be achieved. After Rothstein's death, Capone called a meeting in New York of the major criminal powers and suggested the logical extension of this policy, a national syndicate to co-ordinate criminal activity. Although the plan was rejected by the mutually suspicious gangs, the meeting did lead to co-operative projects like the execution service later known as "Murder Incorporated" and the national illegal betting service that was to provide the gangs' main income after the repeal of prohibition.

The gangs' new standing in national society was reflected in films that showed crime as a highly organised industry. Warner Brothers, experts in entertaining the masses, had produced many of the biographical gangster films: *Little Caesar,* based on Capone; *The Public Enemy,* based on Hymie Weiss; as well as many others. The first all-sound film, *The Lights of New York* (Bryan Foy, 1928) was also drawn from the *genre* that Warners recognised as a potential gold mine. A glance at the newspapers gave their writers dozens of plots, particularly when, after repeal, the gangs moved in on prostitution (*Marked Woman*), the cab business (*Taxi*), trucking, banking, politics. Often imitated by other studios but seldom anticipated, Warners pioneered the private detective film, the prison drama and most of the sub-sections that make up the modern crime film.

* * *

While Hollywood explored the possibilities of organised crime, another pheno- menon was catching public interest. This was the rise of the rural bandits, independent bank-robbers, kidnappers and petty thieves thrown up by the Depression who briefly ravaged the Midwest and South in 1933 and 1934. Racing across Oklahoma, Ohio, Kansas, Missouri and Arkansas, they struck at isolated banks and filling stations in daring daylight raids, often shooting up buildings and people with sub-machine guns before roaring off in their stolen cars. Mostly small-town sports and embittered petty criminals, they traded on a corrupt and inefficient state police force to satisfy their simple needs, money, excitement and fame.

With the possible exception of John Dillinger, these bandits—"Ma" Barker and her sons, Charles "Pretty Boy" Floyd, Bonnie Parker and Clyde Barrow, George "Machine Gun" Kelly, Lester Gillis ("Baby Face" Nelson) and the rest—stole only a tiny percentage of the money that Capone and his associates looted from the country. The gangs looked on them contemptuously as small-time thieves, thrill- seekers and freaks. Their notoriety stemmed solely from their value as news subjects, and the bloody child-like violence of their lives. The Depression society, weary of corruption in government and apathy in business, welcomed the stories of banks held up and policemen baffled. It was not, after all, their money in the banks, and few public servants had proved themselves as corrupt and useless as the state police. Flattered by newspaper attention and their legendary status, the bandits responded, writing to the papers and the officers who hunted them, appearing casually in town to buy food, returning home to visit friends and family, gestures of their contempt for the impotent police force.

This arrogance was their downfall. Left to compete solely with the state police, most of them would have lived for years, but their growing popularity encouraged the Federal authorities to intervene. Given sweeping powers by Congress after the Lindbergh kidnapping, the F.B.I., with its biblically righteous leader J. Edgar Hoover, swept down on the bandits, and within a few months in 1934 most were dead, pursued with icy determination across America by the G-men and shot down with dubious legality by men who knew they had nothing to lose. In 1933, at the height of the hunt, the Production Code authority issued an order that no film on Dillinger, or by implication any of the other bandits, should be made. No longer nourished by publicity, the legends died, not to be revived for another thirty years.

With the big crime rings, Hoover kept an uneasy truce. Even his power was unequal to that of the gangs, and to attack them would be to invite a costly battle that might eventually lead the F.B.I. into the same disrepute as the state police. His neutralisation of Capone in 1931 had merely been the end of a process begun by the gangs, who found Capone's rule galling. Beyond that, Hoover dared not go. Crime films, reflecting this agreement, became panegyrics to the fearless G-men, stories of prison, of racketeering on the city level with civic groups or alert police smashing the small gangs, or individual stories of crime and retribution peopled by private eyes and gentleman gangsters who were already becoming figures of heroic mythopoetry, conveniently distant from the real facts of national graft and corruption.

*　　*　　*

The reality of war and of organised crime burst on the U.S. at roughly the same time. In the Thirties, special investigator Thomas A. Dewey set about cleaning up New York, convicting Mafia leaders and deporting criminal heads. Continuing this work in 1939, other investigators found during a probe into crime in Brooklyn that "the big fix" extended far deeper than anybody had realised. A small-time killer named Abe Reles admitted that for years he had been a paid assassin for a criminal group that carried out executions for the nation's gangs, the group that became known as "Murder Incorporated." His testimony uncovered evidence of gambling, prostitution and union rackets covering the whole country, of corruption extending into government on all levels, into the state and federal police, into industry.

War and America's growing involvement in it blunted the effect of these revelations, and diverted Hollywood from making films based on them. It was not until 1946 that the first films on criminal corruption emerged, and when they did it was with a precision and power that nobody had expected. Many of them reflected the socialist/ humanist views of men who had been attracted to Communism during the periods of Soviet reconstruction in the Thirties and the wartime *entente*. Few of these productions were more fiery than the political parables of Warner Brothers in the early Thirties, e.g. *Wild Boys of the Road,* but the Depression was gone and with it the memory of injustice and graft. In the post-war mood of relaxation, optimism and nostalgia, the realism of *The Naked City, Brute Force, Force of Evil, Body and Soul* and *Crossfire* forced social awareness and civic indignation once again on a careless public, and the world's filmgoers turned with new interest to Hollywood.

Regretfully, the liberal spirit of the time was ephemeral, giving way abruptly to a more typical isolationism and xenophobia. The men whose talents had made these films great—Dassin, Dmytryk, Polonsky, Rossen, Trumbo, Garfield, Hayden—were first to suffer in the McCarthy witch-hunts of the early Fifties, and the spring of social comment that had welled briefly to the surface sank below once more, not to return for many years.

*   *   *

Despite the frankness of these socialist-oriented films, they had little effect on public opinion towards organised crime, now an invisible industry of immense influence and wealth. Since the Forties, the small mobs had been quietly consolidating themselves into a loose confederation of independent area groups with the Italian/Jewish Mafia as informal link. In New York, a committee of Joe Adonis, Willy and Solly Moretti, Albert Anastasia and Anthony "Tony Bender" Strollo met at Duke's Restaurant near Palisades Park through the war, planning strategy and maintaining the "Murder Incorporated" and Continental Press Service gambling machinery. The press ignored crime, but it was widely understood that a "Combination" of top gangsters ran the rackets in America. Gordon Wiles's *The Gangster* (1947) was one of the first films to call it "The Syndicate."

The word became the accepted one for organised crime in 1952, when Senator Estes Kefauver published the findings of the Senate Special Committee to Investigate Crime In Interstate Commerce, of which he was chairman from May 1950 to May 1951. "A nationwide crime syndicate does exist in the United States of America," he announced in a widely-quoted report, and went on, "This nationwide syndicate is a loosely organised but cohesive coalition of autonomous crime 'locals' which work together for mutual profit. Behind the local mobs which make up the national crime syndicate is a shadowy criminal organisation known as the Mafia." Once again, as in 1939, the public was made aware that crime had become far more than a matter of

The Fifties spawned a rash of exposés that purported to tell the truth about graft in a number of cities. Some, like *The Phenix City Story*, were honest attempts to show how apathy led to corruption. Others—*Chicago Syndicate, New Orleans Uncensored, The City Is Dark/Crime Wave, Kansas City Confidential, Hoodlum Empire, The Case against Brooklyn*—settled for a trite formula in which a crusading cop or private citizen shows that behind the well-cut suit of some local dignitary is a gang boss with contacts in the Mafia or the mobs. Respecting the F.B.I.'s truce with big-time crime, these films confined themselves to corruption on a city level, limiting any reference to national organisation to a veiled comment that the Syndicate or "The Big Boy" was worried. Lacking film-makers of social consciousness, the crime film degenerated into another aspect of the Hollywood experience, distinguishable from the cowboy and horror film only in the variety of its attitudes and realism of its settings.

*   *   *

Genres rise and fall, fertilising the ground for new growth, and the gangster film today has been ploughed back to nourish the James Bond cycle, with its suave super-crooks and elaborate gadgetry, or the smooth professionalism of "big caper" films like *Robbery* or *The Split*. Films about fantastic robberies, most of them inspired by real-life crimes like the Brinks armoured car robbery or the Great Train Robbery in England, have become so common that the best of them—*Rififi, The Asphalt Jungle, The Big Caper*—are a sub-*genre* of their own, with special rules deriving more from the imagination of their writers than the realism of the news. As scenarist vies with scenarist to work out more elaborate plots, the underworld looks on, notebook ready, in case one comes up with a new wrinkle.

That the cinema should have become the criminal's university is particularly appropriate. For decades crime and film have had a close and mutually responsible relationship. Not only has the cinema played to crime by recording and glorifying its activities, but criminals have responded with interest to the pictures painted of them. Capone demanded that he be consulted over the script of *Scarface,* and actors from George Raft to Alain Delon have been unwilling to draw a line between their screen *personae* and real life. Films like *Yokel Boy* (1942) with Albert Dekker as a gangster invited to star in a film of his own life, *The Hollywood Story* (1950) where Richard

Craig Stevens as private eye Peter Gunn in GUNN

512-68

Steve McQueen in BULLITT

Conte solves a Twenties murder while directing a film about it, are no more odd than *Broadway* (1942), starring George Raft as himself in a film that often looks and sounds like a Thirties gangster romance. Both in the public eye, both dependent on the protection of their charisma to survive in an uncertain world, both doomed to short-lived careers, gangsters and actors seem too close for true separation.

Tied to the period that creates it, the gangster film has no more durability than the year from which it springs. For this reason today's crime films are thin. The poorest are rooted in nostalgia, pastel memoirs of Forties detective dramas or thin parodies of a *genre* that in its time was brisk and relevant. Others, like *Madigan*, record without comment the commonplace brutality of the city streets and hope for some truth about our time to emerge from the grim catalogue. But in truth the gangster film seems gone for good, as the gangster is gone. With the trench-coat replaced by the well-cut suit, the prison pallor by a Palm Springs tan and guns by more subtle means of persuasion, he has passed beyond the area where cinema could say anything about him except that he once existed, and gave rise to some of the American cinema's most powerful dramas.

Main Entries

1 ADLER, JAY. American actor, thinner, pouchier and more sinister version of his brother Luther. Widely represented in Fifties gangster films as henchman and hood.

Films: *Cry Danger, The Mob/Remember That Face, My Six Convicts, 99 River Street, The Long Wait, Down Three Dark Streets, Vice Squad, Scandal Sheet* (1952)/*The Dark Page, The Big Combo, Illegal, The Killing.*

2 ADLER, LUTHER (1903–). Expert in sweating and cowering, Adler, a pudgy Jewish bullfrog, usually gets rubbed out early in his gangster films. His most bizarre death was in *The Brotherhood*, where Kirk Douglas lets him strangle himself for murdering the former's father.

Films: *Cornered, D.O.A., Kiss Tomorrow Goodbye, M* (1951), *Hoodlum Empire, The Miami Story, Crashout, The Brotherhood.*

3 ALDRICH, ROBERT (1918–). American director, assistant to Losey and heir to some of the Forties' civilised violence and social comment. Recently, however, has been *meneur de jeu* to a series of sado-gerontophilic fantasies like *Whatever Happened to Baby Jane?*

Films: As assistant director: *Body and Soul, Force of Evil, M* (1951), *The Prowler.* As director: *Kiss Me Deadly* (also produced), *The Garment Jungle* (finished by Vincent Sherman after disagreement; all but a few minutes is Aldrich, though Sherman gets the credit).

4 ANKRUM, MORRIS (1904–). Serviceable American character actor often as cop or victim in gangster films.

Films: *Hot Spot/I Wake Up Screaming, The Thin Man Goes Home, The Lady in the Lake, Undercover Girl, The High Wall, Borderline, The Damned Don't Cry, Crashout, When Gangland Strikes.*

5 ANDREWS, DANA (1912–   ).
Clean-cut American leading man whose
memorable Joe Lilac in *Ball of Fire* is a
clever piece of spoof mobsterdom. In
Laura he was the detective haunted by the
hallucinating face of Gene Tierney, and
in most other films a similarly bemused or
victimised hero.

Films: *Ball of Fire, Fallen Angel,
Boomerang, Where the Sidewalk Ends,
While the City Sleeps, Beyond a Reason-
able Doubt.*

Edward Arnold in
EYES IN THE NIGHT

6 ARNOLD, EDWARD (1890–1956).
Sturdy U.S. actor, master of civilised
menace, expert impersonator of the
gangster/executive. In *Three on a Match*
he is the gang boss first seen grotesquely
enlarged in a shaving mirror as he trims
the hairs in his nose. In later films he was
more portly and sympathetic as detective
and *bon viveur* Nero Wolfe in *Meet Nero
Wolfe* and *The League of Frightened Men*,
and a blind investigator in *Eyes in the
Night* and *The Hidden Eye.*

Films: *Afraid to Talk, I Am a Fugitive
from a Chain Gang, Three on a Match,
Whistling in the Dark/Scared, Hideout,
Million Dollar Ransom, The Glass Key*
(1935), *Meet Nero Wolfe, The League of
Frightened Men, The Earl of Chicago, The
Penalty* (1941), *Johnny Apollo, Johnny
Eager, Eyes in the Night, The Hidden Eye,
The City That Never Sleeps, The Houston
Story, Miami Exposé.*

7 ARTHUR, JEAN (1908–   ).
Resourceful Thirties blonde, and foil to
William Powell before Myrna Loy turned
up, she will always be remembered as
Edward G. Robinson's quick-witted
helper in John Ford's *The Whole Town's
Talking.*

Films: *The Canary Murder Case, The
Greene Murder Case, The Gang Buster,
The Defense Rests, The Whole Town's
Talking, Public Hero No. 1, The Ex Mrs.
Bradford, Adventure in Manhattan.*

8 ASTOR, MARY (1906–   ).
Aristocratic U.S. leading lady, most
impressive as the ambiguous heroine of
Huston's *The Maltese Falcon.*

Films: *Romance of the Underworld,
Ladies Love Brutes, The Kennel Murder
Case, The Case of the Howling Dog, The
Little Giant, I Am a Thief, The Murder of
Dr. Harrigan, The Maltese Falcon* (1941).

Mary Astor and Humphrey Bogart in THE MALTESE FALCON

9 ATTENBOROUGH, RICHARD (1923–). Before he entered production and direction, this skilled English actor added some fine portraits to the urban rogues' gallery: a pimply and vicious thug in the film of Graham Greene's *Brighton Rock,* lecherous and flippant mechanic in *The League of Gentlemen,* part of a strange kidnap plot in *Seance on a Wet Afternoon* and a smooth con man in *Only When I Larf.*

10 BACALL, LAUREN (1924–). The most beautiful of Howard Hawks's creations, a twenty-year-old model whom he turned into one of the Forties' most hallucinating stars. The smoky voice, shouted down to permanent huskiness in the Hollywood hills, drifts over the years, an evocative memory of the period when Bogart reigned.

Films: *The Big Sleep, Dark Passage, Key Largo, Harper/The Moving Target.*

Lauren Bacall and Humphrey Bogart in DARK PASSAGE

11 BACON, LLOYD (1889–1955). One of the second-line Warners directors of the Thirties, lacking the brilliance of Curtiz and LeRoy but showing nevertheless a polished technique and acid wit.

Films: *Fingerprints, Brass Knuckles, Miss Pinkerton, Picture Snatcher, A Very Honorable Guy, 'Frisco Kid, Marked Woman, San Quentin* (1937), *A Slight Case of Murder, Racket Busters, Invisible Stripes, Brother Orchid, Larceny Inc.*

12 BAKER, STANLEY (1928–   ). Stocky Welsh actor of tough-guy roles, and lately producer. Expert as embittered men: larcenous sergeant robbing army camp in *A Prize of Arms*, tough old lag in *The Criminal*, cynical cop of *Blind Date/Chance Meeting* and *Hell Is a City*.

Films: *Undercover, The Good Die Young, Hell Drivers, Violent Playground, Blind Date/Chance Meeting, Hell Is a City, The Criminal, A Prize of Arms, Robbery* (also produced).

13 BANCROFT, GEORGE (1882–1956). Josef von Sternberg's caption to the picture of Bancroft in his autobiography reads, "*Underworld* (1927), the first gangster film. This is Bull Weed, lawbreaker, who once said to me: 'I know why you are fond of directing me. You want to be like me, don't you?'" The quote says a great deal about both men. The burly U.S. actor repeated his role in a number of Thirties gangster films, but never lived up to his portrait of reasoned brutality in *Underworld*.

Films: *Underworld, Docks of New York, The Showdown, The Dragnet, Thunderbolt, Ladies Love Brutes, The Mighty, Scandal Sheet* (1931), *Blood Money, Racketeers in Exile, Angels with Dirty Faces, Each Dawn I Die.*

14 BARKER, ARIZONA CLARK ("Ma") (1880–1935).

"The eyes of Arizona Clark Barker always fascinated me. They were queerly direct, penetrating, hot with some strangely smouldering flame, yet withal as hypnotically cold as the muzzle of a gun. That same dark mysterious brilliance was in the eyes of her four sons." Like most things said about "Ma" Barker and her boys, J. Edgar Hoover's tribute is probably based on legend. He may never have seen any of the family: of the four Barker boys, Herman was found dead in 1927, either a suicide or dead of wounds sustained in a robbery, Arthur drew a life sentence for murder in 1928, and Lloyd twenty-five years in Leavenworth for mail robbery around the same time.

The fourth, Freddie, called "Dock", was associated with the others in their early careers, but hardly progressed

Stanley Baker (left) in ROBBERY

beyond robbery, burglary and assault until the early Thirties. Then with his mother, her lover Arthur Dunlop and gunman Alvin "Creepy" Karpis, he carried out a series of smooth bank raids in Kansas, Missouri and Minnesota, "Ma" acting as scout and cover. Their downfall, like that of the other rural bandits, came from carrying out a Federal crime, the kidnapping of bank president Edward G. Bremer of St. Paul. G-men tracked the gang to a luxuriously furnished holiday home at Lake Weir, near Oklawaha, Fla., where "Ma" and Freddie died in a furious machine gun battle on January 16, 1935.

Not often shown on film, the story of the Barkers was done best as an episode of the TV series *The Untouchables* with Claire Trevor as "Ma," but Blanche Yurka was a savage surrogate in *Queen of the Mob* (1940) and the character was also shown in the feature based on the *Gangbusters* TV series, *Guns Don't Argue* (1955). Latest study: *Bloody Mama* by Roger Corman, with Shelley Winters as "Ma."

15 BARROW, CLYDE (1910–1934) and **PARKER, BONNIE** (–1934) ("Bonnie & Clyde"). No legend of banditry has so far outrun reality as that of Bonnie and Clyde, represented in many films, most notably Arthur Penn's

Shelley Winters (centre) as "Ma" Barker in Roger Corman's production of BLOODY MAMA

Warren Beatty and Faye Dunaway in BONNIE AND CLYDE

1968 *Bonnie and Clyde,* as star-crossed lovers of poetic significance. The real story, of a small-town sport and his shrewish mistress, is less glamorous, though in its own way grimly moving.

Clyde "Buck" Barrow and his brother

End of Bonnie and Clyde : still from
THE BONNIE PARKER STORY

Marvin Ivan ("Ivy") climaxed an early career of petty crime around their home town of West Dallas, Texas, when they were arrested for car stealing in January 1930. "Buck" got two years, "Ivy" four. Released in February 1932 as part of a general parole, they split up, and Clyde began an independent career. A month after his release he robbed a service station, two months after release he shot John Bucher, a merchant in Hillsboro, Texas, and five months after that shot two men in a dance hall in Atoka, Okla. One died, and Clyde's companion, Roy Hamilton, was arrested. When he was jailed, Clyde teamed up with his friend's mistress, Kansas City waitress Bonnie Parker.

Bonnie and Clyde pulled a few Texas robberies, then rescued Hamilton from jail in a daring raid on a work party outside the prison walls. In December 1932, the three joined up with "Ivy" Barrow and his wife, Blanche Caldwell, pulling a series of small bank hold-ups in Texas and the Midwest. The gang were trapped and nearly captured on January 7, 1933, but shot their way out. On July 24, at Dexter, Iowa, "Ivy" was fatally wounded, and Bonnie and Clyde continued their activities until ambushed at Shreveport, La., on May 23, 1934, and shot to death.

Most film-makers have declined to consider the couple as they really were, a sadist and his moll. ("Residents of Houston Heights, who were neighbours of Clyde Barrow when he resided there as a boy, recalled today he had gotten into trouble several times for torturing pet

22

animals. Clyde, they said, would break a bird's wing, then laugh at its attempts to fly." *New York Times,* May 24, 1934.) Instead they convey the image of a young couple set against a hostile establishment, ranging the rural farmlands of the mid-west searching as much for themselves as for plunder.

The legend began with Fritz Lang's *You Only Live Once* (1937) which, while not a true parallel, was suggested by the incident. Henry Fonda and Sylvia Sidney were a couple condemned by social injustice to a short-lived career of crime. More fanciful, Joseph H. Lewis in *Gun Crazy* (1949) set John Dall's handsome gun fetishist—"Shooting guns is what I want to do when I grow up. I don't know why but I feel good when I'm shooting 'em"—against Peggy Cummins's sexy side-show sharpshooter in a story derived from the legend, conveying by brilliant technique (a robbery shown in one take from the back seat of a car, superb evocation of the rural midwest's emptiness) an unlikely but poetic core to the relationship.

Closer to the facts, *The Bonnie Parker Story* (1958) was false mainly in the tinselled glamour of Dorothy Provine as the heroine. But her Clyde was brainless, rustic and impotent, as in real life, and the background grimly devoid of poetry. It was left to Arthur Penn to set the legend firmly in ascendancy over the truth, perpetuating it in an age weary of legends by stressing its modern aspects. Warren Beatty and Faye Dunaway (a pity Tuesday Weld was prevented by her pregnancy from taking the role written for her) look as glossily romantic as the film-stars they so obviously are, and embody the dreams of adolescence—the sexually frustrated boy who "makes out," the girl who dies a legend. One accepts the rich colour, the humour, the

gleeful violence without once relating it to real life. Only in the scene of Bonnie visiting her mother and, in the midst of a family picnic, being reminded of her mortality, does the film hint at the truth behind this strange couple.

Also *Persons in Hiding* (1938), *Guns Don't Argue* (1955).

16 BAXTER, WARNER (1892–1951). Talented U.S. actor seldom given the chance to display his skill, being most often confined to routine programme pictures, like the "Crime Doctor" series in which he played a forensic investigator.

Films: *The Great Gatsby* (1926), *The Crime Doctor, The Crime Doctor's Courage, The Crime Doctor's Gamble, The Crime Doctor's Diary, The Crime Doctor's Warning, The Crime Doctor's Manhunt, The Millerson Case* (same series), *Prison Warden, State Penitentiary.*

17 BEAUDINE, WILLIAM (1892–1970). One is always surprised that this director, king of the Forties' Z-pictures, should have directed Mary Pickford in *Sparrows* (1926) and handled some of the best W. C. Fields and Harry Langdon comedies. His crime melodramas, always professional, show little of this initial promise.

Films: *The Crime of the Century, Torchy Gets Her Man, Torchy Blane in Chinatown, Federal Fugitives, Desperate Cargo, Phantom Killer, Men of San Quentin, Black Market Babies, Blonde Ransom, Killer at Large, The Feathered Serpent, Jail Busters.*

18 BECKER, JACQUES (1906–1960). French director, assistant to Renoir and creator of some important films which combine French perception with American pace.

Films: *Touchez Pas au Grisbi, The*

Adventures of Arsène Lupin, Le Trou/The Hole.

19 BEERY, WALLACE (1889–1949). Lumbering U.S. actor whose simple skills were used by George Hill when he cast him as the prison ring-leader in *The Big House* and as a prototype Capone in *The Secret Six*. Von Sternberg was less successful and his performance as the New York cop in *Sergeant Madden* added little to a muddled film.

20 BEGLEY, ED (1901–1970). Brilliant U.S. character actor whose role as the shrill bigot in Lumet's *Twelve Angry Men*

is the focus of the harrowing final scene. Also impressive as the gang leader in *The Turning Point* and a card hustler strangled and suffocated in a curtain in *Dark City*. His brand of beady-eyed menace is probably impossible to better.

Films: *Boomerang, The Street with No Name, The Great Gatsby* (1949), *Backfire, Convicted, Dark City, On Dangerous Ground, The Turning Point, Odds against Tomorrow, Warning Shot.*

21 BELLAMY, RALPH (1904–   ). A convincing Ellery Queen, smooth unraveller of complex crimes, Bellamy

Wallace Beery (right) with Chester Morris and Robert Montgomery in THE BIG HOUSE

24

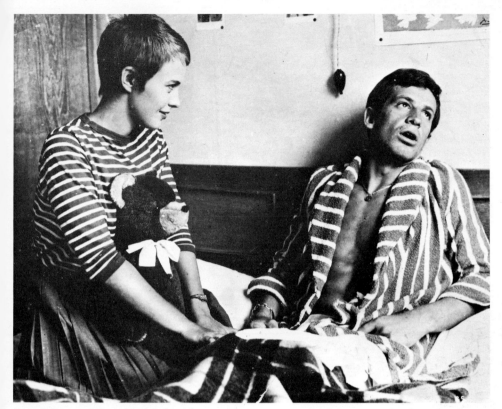

Jean Seberg and Jean-Paul Belmondo
in A BOUT DE SOUFFLE/BREATHLESS

also created on stage the role of McLeod in Sidney Kingsley's *Detective Story* which Kirk Douglas took in Wyler's film.

Films: *The Secret Six, Illicit, Disorderly Conduct, Parole Girl, Picture Snatcher, Brother Orchid, Ellery Queen Master Detective, Queen of the Mob, Ellery Queen's Penthouse Mystery, Ellery Queen's Perfect Crime, Ellery Queen and the Murder Ring, Eyes of the Underworld.*

22 BELMONDO, JEAN-PAUL (1933–). Although some French critics have called Belmondo a combination of

Cagney, Bogart, Fonda *and* Gabin, his actual standing is less derivative, and less strong. He was Bogart-like in *Classe Tous Risques/The Big Risk,* more so in *Le Doulos/The Finger Man,* but his thoughtful *fin de siècle* thief in Malle's *Le Voleur* owed nothing to any model.

Films: *Classe Tous Risques/The Big Risk, À Bout de Souffle/Breathless, Un Nommé la Rocca/A Man Named Rocca, Le Doulos/The Finger Man, L'Aîné des Ferchaux/Magnet of Doom, Cent Mille Dollars au Soleil/Greed in the Sun, Le Cerveau/The Brain, Borsalino.*

25

23 BENDIX, WILLIAM (1907–1964). Homely gravel-voiced U.S. actor who could play both brute and Babe Ruth. As a heavy, his Neanderthal implacability made it clear at a glance that he was open neither to bribes nor reason; best roles as the white-suited torpedo in Hathaway's *The Dark Corner* and the brutal escaped convict in *Crashout*.

Films: *The Glass Key* (1943), *The Blue Dahlia, The Dark Corner, Race Street, The Big Steal, Detective Story, Gambling House, Macao, Dangerous Mission, Crashout, The Rough and the Smooth* (in U.K.).

William Bendix (above) in THE DARK CORNER

24 BENEDEK, LASLO (1907–). Hungarian-born director who made a minor U.S. reputation for off-beat dramas. Best remembered for crisp direction of *The Wild One* and equally smooth rendering of Arthur Miller's *Death of a Salesman*. In *Port of New York* a hirsute Yul Brynner is king of a drug-smuggling racket.

Films: *Port of New York, The Wild One, Moment of Danger* (in U.K.).

25 BEZZERIDES, A. I. U.S. scriptwriter, among the most talented of the Forties but prevented, like Abraham Polonsky, from adequately displaying his talent.

Films: *They Drive by Night, Juke Girl, Thieves' Highway, On Dangerous Ground, Kiss Me Deadly, A Bullet for Joey* (with Geoffrey Homes).

26 BICKFORD, CHARLES (1892–1969). Thin-lipped white-haired U.S. heavy, seldom cast any more sympathetically than as the harassed studio boss in *A Star Is Born* or the ulcer-ridden gambler in *Mr. Cory*. In DeMille's *This Day and Age* he was a murderer held by a gang of teenage vigilantes over a pit of rats to elicit a confession, and things did not improve much after that.

Films: *Song of the Eagle, Little Miss Marker, Gangs of New York, Street of Missing Men, Mutiny in the Big House, Butch Minds the Baby, Mr. Lucky, Fallen Angel, The Dark Corner, Brute Force, Mr. Cory.*

27 BLONDELL, JOAN (1909–). Cleverest and most attractive of Warner's Thirties blondes, apt foil to Cagney in his first film, *Sinner's Holiday,* and in *The Public Enemy,* where she was part of a *ménage à quatre* with Cagney and friends.

Films: *Illicit, The Public Enemy, Miss*

Charles Bickford (centre) with Hume Cronyn,
Ray Teal, and Sam Levene in BRUTE FORCE

Pinkerton, Big City Blues, Three on a
Match, Lawyer Man, Broadway Bad,
Bullets or Ballots, Cry Havoc, The Corpse
Came C.O.D.

28 BOGART, HUMPHREY (1899–
1957). All the best things have already
been written about Bogart. There is
nothing left to say except that nobody
more completely epitomised the character of the urban wolf, nor so effectively
conveyed the spirit of *film noir*. "Bogart
is so much better than any other tough-
guy actor. (He) can be tough *without* a
gun. Also he has a sense of humour that

contains that grating undertone of contempt."—Raymond Chandler.

Films: *Up the River* (1930), *Three on a*
Match, Midnight (1934), *The Petrified*
Forest, Bullets or Ballots, Marked Woman,
Kid Galahad (1937), *San Quentin* (1937),
Dead End, Crime School, The Amazing
Dr. Clitterhouse, Racket Busters, Angels
with Dirty Faces, King of the Underworld,
You Can't Get Away with Murder, The
Roaring Twenties, Invisible Stripes, It All
Came True, Brother Orchid, They Drive
by Night, High Sierra, The Maltese
Falcon (1941), *All through the Night, The*
Big Shot, The Big Sleep, Dark Passage,

Humphrey Bogart
in DEAD END

Key Largo, Knock on Any Door, The Enforcer/Murder Inc., Beat the Devil, We're No Angels, The Desperate Hours.

29 BORGNINE, ERNEST (1917–   ). Even in *Marty*, Borgnine was hardly lovable, and his beer-belly, coarse laugh and subtly sadistic features have made him in other films a born heavy. An interesting exception was *Pay or Die* where, as the turn-of-the-century New York Italian cop probing the Mafia, he conveyed earnest good humour and Mediterranean cunning in a clever performance.

Films: *The Mob/Remember That Face, Bad Day at Black Rock, Violent Saturday, Pay or Die, The Split.*

30 BRAND, NEVILLE (1920–   ). American actor, stock menace in score of

routine films. Too dapper as Capone in *The Scarface Mob* and *The George Raft Story/Spin of a Coin*, pockmarked war hero Brand shone best as the honourable convict representative in *Riot in Cell Block 11*, skilled mouthpiece for ex-convict producer Walter Wanger's indignant remarks on prison brutality and neglect, and the Detroit torpedo who rubs out William Holden at the fights in *The Turning Point*.

Films: *D.O.A., Where the Sidewalk Ends, The Mob/Remember That Face, The Turning Point, Kansas City Confidential, The Secret Four, Riot in Cell Block 11, Man Crazy, Cry Terror, The Way to the Gold, The Scarface Mob, The George Raft Story/Spin of a Coin, Birdman of Alcatraz.*

31 BRIAN, DAVID (1914–   ). Suave U.S. actor with a good line in smooth criminals. He led Joan Crawford astray in *The Damned Don't Cry*.

Films: *The Damned Don't Cry, The Great Jewel Robber, Inside the Walls of Folsom Prison, This Woman Is Dangerous, The Accused, A Pocketful of Miracles.*

32 BRONSON, CHARLES (1920–   ). Polish-American heavy, best remembered as an uncomplicated "Machine Gun" Kelly in Corman's film. Early work as Charles Buchinski.

Films: *My Six Convicts, The City Is Dark/Crime Wave, Big House U.S.A., Machine Gun Kelly, Gang War, Kid Galahad* (1962).

33 BROOK, CLIVE (1891–   ). Phlegmatic British actor, in U.S. from the early silent days. His best role, aside from playing Sherlock Holmes in some early sound versions, was as "Rolls" Royce in Von Sternberg's *Underworld*, a brilliant and moving cameo.

Clive Brook
in FORGOTTEN FACES

and N.Y.U. degrees, his films show a deep involvement in the issues of his time reminiscent of that shown by Mark Hellinger. His quick temper—he was known all over Hollywood as "the director who socked a producer"—led to him being taken off some films, denied others.

Films: Original story: *The Doorway to Hell, Boy of the Streets, Angels with Dirty Faces, Nocturne* (with Frank Fenton), *Kanas City Confidential.* As screen writer: *State's Attorney.* As director: *Quick Millions* (also wrote), *Hell's Highway* (also part wrote), *Blood Money* (also wrote), *The Devil Is a Sissy* (replaced by W. S. Van Dyke during shooting).

36   BURNETT, WILLIAM R. (1899–   ). American screen-writer and novelist, creator of the original *Little Caesar* and writer on such vital gangster films as *The Asphalt Jungle* and *High Sierra.* Notable for his clear unromantic view of crime which showed itself whether in the energy of *Little Caesar* or the moving realism of his Western novel on the Holliday/Earp friendship filmed as *Law and Order* (1932).

Films: Original story: *Little Caesar* (from his own novel), *The Finger Points, The Beast of the City, Scarface* (with Seton I. Miller, John Lee Mahin and Ben Hecht), *Dark Hazard, The Whole Town's Talking, 36 Hours to Kill, Some Blondes Are Dangerous, King of the Underworld, High Sierra, Accused of Murder, The Accused, I Died a Thousand Times* (remake of *High Sierra*). As screen-writer: *This Gun for Hire, The Asphalt Jungle, The Racket* (1951) (from Bartlett Cormack play), *Dangerous Mission* (with Horace McCoy and Charles Bennett), *Illegal* (with James R. Webb).

Films: *The Penalty* (1920), *Underworld, Forgotten Faces, Scandal Sheet* (1931).

34   BROOKS, RICHARD (1912–   ). U.S. director, novelist and screen-writer. A thoughtful, exact technician, reminiscent of David Lean in his fascination with the mechanics of simple relationships under stress. His novel *The Producer* is based on the life of Mark Hellinger, and another book, *The Brick Foxhole,* was filmed as *Crossfire.*

Films: as screen-writer: *Mystery Street, Key Largo, Any Number Can Play.* As director: *The Blackboard Jungle, In Cold Blood.*

35   BROWN, ROWLAND (1900–   ). U.S. screen-writer/director with blighted career. A pressman with Yale

37   BURR, RAYMOND (1917–   ). Undemonstrative and burly U.S. heavy,

James Cagney (left) with Humphrey Bogart in ANGELS WITH DIRTY FACES

most famous as Perry Mason and crippled detective Ironside in the TV series of those names.

Films: *San Quentin* (1946), *Desperate, Raw Deal, Red Light, Borderline, M* (1951), *His Kind of Woman, F.B.I. Girl, Meet Danny Wilson, A Cry in the Night, P.J./New Face in Hell.*

38 CAGNEY, JAMES (1904–   ). "No one expresses more clearly in terms of pictorial action the delights of violence, the overtones of a semi-conscious sadism, the tendency towards destruction, towards anarchy, which is the basis of American sex-appeal." (Lincoln Kirstein).

Pugnacious little taxi-drivers and energetic gunmen were Cagney's specialties, although he began as a Broadway and Hollywood dancer. Brought up on New York's East Side, he never, not even in his most sympathetic roles, lost the mannerisms of the gangster, the staccato delivery, the curling lip, the odd hitch of the trousers with his clenched fists. (Asked to explain the latter in a Forties "Inside Hollywood" picture, he grinned, opened his coat, and said, "Easy. No belt.")

An ambitious talent and willingness to work at unconventional parts has led him into some odd situations; the reformed alcoholic in *Come Fill the Cup,* ex-con.

governor of a prison farm in *The Mayor of Hell,* and the harassed Berlin representative of Coca Cola in Wilder's *One Two Three.* In all these, his cardinal rule for acting, "Never relax," has seldom let him down, although his set-pieces—screaming "Top of the world, ma!" as he empties his gun into a spherical gas tank in *White Heat;* squashing a grapefruit in Mae Clark's face in *The Public Enemy*—sometimes obscure the moment in *Angels with Dirty Faces* where he harmonises with the choir in his old church, or the climactic scenes of his own production, the vicious and uncompromising *Kiss Tomorrow Goodbye.* The success of the latter, and of *Short Cut to Hell,* the remake of *This Gun for Hire* that Cagney directed, show a shrewd and sensitive film artist. Although restricted in range and condemned by a set of crude superficial mannerisms to be every impressionist's butt, Cagney has ornamented a long career with some legitimate gems.

Films: as director: *Short Cut to Hell.* As actor: *The Doorway to Hell, The Millionaire, The Public Enemy, Smart Money, Blonde Crazy, Taxi* (1932), *Hard to Handle, The Mayor of Hell, G-Men, Angels with Dirty Faces, Each Dawn I Die, The Roaring Twenties, White Heat, Kiss Tomorrow Goodbye* (also produced), *Love Me Or Leave Me, Never Steal Anything Small.*

39 CAHN, EDWARD L. (1899–1963). Prolific U.S. director of Z-films, many with crime subjects.

Films: *Homicide Squad, Radio Patrol, Afraid to Talk, Main Street after Dark, Experiment Alcatraz* (also produced), *The Great Plane Robbery, Girls in Prison, Guns Girls and Gangsters, Riot in a Juvenile Prison, Inside the Mafia.* Also many shorts in *Crime Does Not Pay* series.

40 CALLEIA, JOSEPH (1887–   ). Maltese-born actor with a long career in U.S. films as henchman. Superbly used by Orson Welles as the corrupt assistant to Quinlan in *Touch of Evil.*

Films: *Public Hero No. 1, Tough Guy, After the Thin Man, Algiers, Full Confession, The Glass Key* (1943), *Lured, The Noose Hangs High, Noose* (U.K.), *Touch of Evil, Cry Tough, Johnny Cool.*

*Joseph Calleia
(below) in TOUCH OF EVIL*

41 CAPONE, AL (Alphonso Caponi) (1895–1947). The king of gangsters, a regional warlord whose control over Chicago and environs was total. Ruthless, amoral, egotistical and cunning, he embodied the essential dichotomy of organised crime: condemned by society for

Still from THE SCARFACE MOB,
directed by Phil Karlson with Neville Brand as Al Capone

his activities he remained by most of its standards a successful and admirable man.

Born in Castel Amaro, near Rome, he came to America with his family as a baby. He soon drifted into crime in New York, where in a bar-room fight with gangster Frank Gallucio he sustained two parallel three-inch scars on his left cheek which were to give him his nickname, "Scarface." In 1921 he was brought to Chicago by Johnny Torrio, boss of the city's largest gang. After good work as a killer and strong-arm man, he eased out Torrio and took over. From 1927 to 1930 he ruled unchecked over the city. Vigilante groups (The Secret Six, among others),

the efforts of the mayor (who named him "Public Enemy No. 1"), and of other gangs could not unseat him. He neutralised Torrio (who, after a murder attempt, retired in 1925), wiped out the North Side Mob and Roger Touhy's Des Plaines gang, his main opponents.

Capone's rule ended abruptly in the first pressure of the Federal purge. In 1929 he was arrested on two minor charges, one for failing to appear as a murder witness to a crime he was obviously not guilty of, and the second for carrying a concealed pistol. While serving short sentences for these, the Federal tax authorities investigated him, as a result of which in October 1931 he was

John Boorman's POINT BLANK. Walker (Lee Marvin) takes an address book from Carter (Lloyd Bochner), whose syndicate has tried to kill him. Photo: M-G-M.

Roger Corman's THE ST. VALENTINE'S DAY MAS-
SACRE. The massacre in the garage. Photo: 20th
Century-Fox.

given an eleven year term for tax evasion. *The Undercover Man* (1949) was based on this historic case. In November 1939, he was released from jail, mad and fatally ill from paresis. He died on January 25, 1947.

Capone played always to the public, conscious of his image as a gang boss. During the Depression he set up soup kitchens in Chicago streets, and offered from jail to have his gang hunt down the Lindbergh kidnapper. While in Atlanta Prison he also heard of plans to film *Scarface,* and demanded that the script be submitted to him for approval. (It is even rumoured that Warner Brothers offered Capone $200,000 to appear in the film, but this is doubtful.) It is an index to his changing image that, when Richard Wilson produced *Al Capone* in 1959, the Capone family, far from being flattered, sued—without success—to have the film stopped.

Though Hawks's *Scarface* with Paul Muni as Tony Camonte is the best Capone film, competition is strong. W. R. Burnett's novel *Little Caesar* was part of an early-Thirties rash of biographies—Edgar Wallace's play *On the Spot*, Ben Hecht's *The Front Page* (filmed by Milestone in 1931) and countless films traded on the legend. *Little Caesar* was filmed by Mervyn LeRoy, and George Hill cast Wallace Beery as a Capone surrogate in *The Secret Six.*

Even after the end of true gangster- om, the character, or parts of it, prospered. Judith Anderson was *Lady Scarface* in 1941, and in *The Gangster* (1947) Barry Sullivan carried Capone's scarred cheek. In the Fifties, the popular TV series *The Untouchables,* based on the efforts of Federal agent Eliot Ness to break the Capone ring, led to *The Scarface Mob,* with Neville Brand as Capone, a role he played again in *The George Raft*

Story/Spin of a Coin, and to Wilson's *Al Capone,* with Rod Steiger as the most convincing Capone since Muni. Jason Robards Jr. played him in *The St. Valentine's Day Massacre.* No doubt there will be others; the figure of Al Capone is one to conjure with in the rogues' gallery of gangsterdom.

42 CAREY, TIMOTHY. Carey's part as the tall soldier executed for cowardice in Kubrick's *Paths of Glory* won praise; most people forget an earlier and more memorable Kubrick role, as the marksman who shoots the horse in *The Killing.* Arguably the least lovable actor since Rondo Hatton, Carey was also the giggling psychopath convict in *House of Numbers* and the murderer in *Revolt in the Big House.* Also *Crime Wave/The City Is Dark, Rumble on the Docks, Convicts Four.*

43 CHANDLER, RAYMOND (1889–1962). The most brilliant of all crime romance writers, creator of the *genre* of private eye films and of the definitive works on which many of the best have been based. His character of Philip Marlowe, quintessential urban wolf, has been interpreted with varying success by Humphrey Bogart, Dick Powell, Robert Montgomery and James Garner. "Embodied in his work is a criticism, at once bitter and sardonic, of a society which, whilst it hounds and pursues the minor criminal, allows the big-shot racketeer . . . the man who can still buy protection from a corrupt police force, and crooked politicians. . . . to go scot-free." (Harry Wilson).

Chandler's Hollywood career was mixed. The screenplays on which he worked, never from his own books, had patches of brilliance, but scripts written by others from his novels seldom conveyed the original spirit. Original story:

Timothy Carey in THE KILLING

Time to Kill (screenplay by Clarence Upson Young). Original screenplays: *Double Indemnity* (with Billy Wilder, from James M. Cain story), *And Now Tomorrow* (with Frank Partos), *The Unseen* (with Hagar Wilde), *The Blue Dahlia, Strangers on a Train* (with Czenzi Ormonde). (In 1947 Chandler wrote a screenplay for Universal—never filmed, it was finally novelised as *Playback*.) Adaptations of his novels to film: *The Falcon Takes Over* (partly from *Farewell My Lovely*), *Murder My Sweet/Farewell My Lovely* (script by John Paxton based on *Farewell My Lovely*), *The Big Sleep* (script by Leigh Brackett, Jules Furth-

man and William Faulkner), *The Brashe Doubloon/The High Window* (script b Dorothy Hannah based on *The Higf Window*), *The Lady in the Lake* (script b Steve Fisher), *Marlowe* (script by Stirling Silliphant based on *The Little Sister*).

44 CHICAGO. Capital of the state o Illinois, and for most of the Twenties and early Thirties the centre of organisec crime in the U.S.A. Detroit was as tougf in its way during the early Twenties, bu Prohibition made Chicago, with its in- dustrial tradition and convenient acces to Canada via the Great Lakes, th criminal pivot of the country. During

A film scripted by Raymond Chandler:
DOUBLE INDEMNITY, with Barbara Stanwyck and Fred MacMurray

Prohibition, Chicago was a criminal enclave, run by the gang bosses with the autocracy of medieval barons.

From 1910 to 1920, the city was controlled by "Big Jim" Colosimo, but on May 11, 1920, he was murdered by associate/employee Johnny Torrio. Small, dapper and intelligent, Torrio instituted a logical division of territory among the gangs, forbade hijacking of liquor shipments and settled conflicts over territory. Those who resisted, like Dion O'Bannion of the North Side Mob, were ruthlessly exterminated, O'Bannion on November 10, 1922, in the famous Flower Shop murder. The killing was engineered by Al Capone, Torrio's lieutenant and later replacement.

Torrio was forced out in 1925, and Capone took over, expanding the empire. The North Side Mob, constantly dissident, was put down in 1926, when its then-leader, Hymie Weiss (basis of the film *The Public Enemy*), was murdered in the same florist where O'Bannion had been killed, and in 1929 at the St. Valentine's Day Massacre, an attempt by Capone and others to wipe out "Bugs" Moran, Weiss's successor. Other evidence connects Capone with the destruction of the Des Plaines Mob, led by Roger "The Terrible" Touhy.

With the imprisonment of Capone in 1931 and the repeal of Prohibition in 1933, control of the depleted rackets passed into the hands of Capone lieutenants Jacob "Greasy Thumb" Gusik and Anthony "The Enforcer" Accardo. When Estes Kefauver investigated Chicago in 1951, he found it a still active centre of illegal operations, but based on gambling and prostitution. In a rare example of criminal sentiment, Chicago gangs were still known as The Capone Syndicate.

The city of Chicago became so linked with organised crime that film-makers automatically used it as a setting, or incorporated the name into films set some distance away. In 1931, when two British gangster films were made at Elstree, they were called *The Man from Chicago* and *The Innocents of Chicago*. *Chicago Digest* was made in Italy, and many others using the word were produced in Hollywood, e.g. *The Earl of Chicago, The Widow from Chicago, Chicago Syndicate,* etc.

See also AL CAPONE, PROHIBITION, THE ST. VALENTINE'S DAY MASSACRE, ROGER TOUHY.

45 CIANNELLI, EDOUARD (1887–1969). Italian actor in many American crime films as heavily-accented gunman or Mafia-style gangster. Was decrepit Mafia don in *The Brotherhood* to great effect.

Films: *Winterset, Marked Woman, Criminal Lawyer* (1937), *The League of Frightened Men, Law of the Underworld, Bulldog Drummond's Bride, The Angels Wash Their Faces, Ellery Queen's Penthouse Mystery, They Got Me Covered, Dillinger, The Crime Doctor's Gamble, I Love Trouble, The Brotherhood.*

46 COBB, LEE J. (1911–   ). Commanding U.S. character actor: Johnny

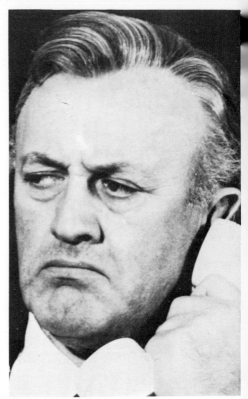

Above : Lee J. Cobb

Friendly, the waterfront racketeer in *On the Waterfront*, and the weary New York detective in *Coogan's Bluff*.

Films: *Boomerang, Johnny O'Clock, Call Northside 777, The Dark Past, Thieves' Highway, The Man Who Cheated Himself, On the Waterfront, The Garment Jungle, Miami Exposé, Party Girl, The Trap/The Baited Trap, They Came To Rob Las Vegas, Coogan's Bluff.*

47 COCHRAN, STEVE (1917–1965). U.S. leading man who looked like a cleaner version of Sheldon Leonard. Often in crime films, his best *The Chase*, where he had a duplicate accelerator installed in the back seat of his limousine and gave his chauffeur some nasty moments. Eventually henchman Peter Lorre takes over the back seat and drives his boss under a train.

Films: *A Song Is Born, White Heat, The Damned Don't Cry, The Chase* (1946), *Highway 301, Inside the Walls of Folsom Prison, Private Hell 36, I Mobster, The Big Operator*.

48 CONRAD, WILLIAM (1920–). Rotund U.S. actor with varied career: radio actor, the voice of Matt Dillon in *Gunsmoke*, movies in Forties and Fifties as burly heavy, then director/producer in Sixties, his best work a brilliant thriller called *Brainstorm*.

Films: as actor: *The Killers* (1945), *Body and Soul, Any Number Can Play,* *One Way Street, Cry Danger, The Racket* (1951), *Five against the House*.

49 CONTE, RICHARD (1919–). U.S. leading man of Italian extraction, star of many crime films. With his toneless voice, disarming smile and a walk like a clockwork toy, he has starred as gangster or detective in a number of important films.

Films: *Somewhere in the Night, Call Northside 777, Cry of the City, Thieves' Highway, The Sleeping City, Under the Gun, Highway Dragnet, Little Red Monkey* (in U.K.), *The Big Tipoff, New York Confidential, The Big Combo, The Brothers Rico, Ocean's Eleven, Assault on a Queen, Tony Rome, Lady in Cement*.

Steve Cochran (at left) in A SONG IS BORN

Richard Conte in LITTLE RED MONKEY ...

50 COOK, ELISHA Jnr. (1907–   ).
American character actor, almost always
cast as victim, dupe or stooge. His
Wilmer, the gunsel in Huston's *The
Maltese Falcon,* is a masterpiece of underplayed malice and thick-headed complicity.

Films : *Grand Jury Secrets, The Maltese
Falcon* (1941), *Hot Spot/I Wake Up
Screaming, The Big Sleep, Dillinger, The
Falcon's Alibi, Two Smart People, The
Gangster, Fall Guy, The Great Gatsby*
(1949), *I the Jury, The Miami Story, The
Killing, Chicago Confidential, Baby Face
Nelson, Plunder Road, Accused of Murder,
Platinum High School/Rich Young and
Deadly, Johnny Cool.*

51 CORMAN, ROGER (1926–   ).
American director/producer/occasional
actor whose lively Z-films transcend their
impoverished resources. His later elegant
fantasies and sociological extensions of
his early beginnings, e.g. *The St. Valentine's Day Massacre,* have fewer delights
than *arcana* like *Rock All Night,* where a
pugnacious half-pint subdues some gangsters in a primitive statement of society's
need for the misfit, or the Corman-pro-
duced *Hot Car Girl* (Bernard Kowalski),
a film of social and cinematic precision.

Films : as director : *Rock All Night,
Machine Gun Kelly, Swamp Women, I
Mobster, The St. Valentine's Day Mas-
sacre.* As producer : *Highway Dragnet.* As

... and HIGHWAY DRAGNET, produced by Roger Corman

Executive Producer: *Stakeout on Dope Street, Cry Baby Killer, Hot Car Girl.*

52 CORTEZ, RICARDO (1899–   ). Austrian-born Jewish actor whose swarthy good looks made him a "Latin lover" in the Thirties, as well as a servicable hood. He was Sam Spade in the first film of *The Maltese Falcon* in 1931, and Napoleonic gang boss "Goldie" Gorio in *Bad Company* (1932). Also had brief spell as a director 1939–1940.

Films: As director: *City of Chance.* As actor: *Chicago, Illicit, The Maltese Falcon/Dangerous Female* (1931), *Bad Company, Broadway Bad, The Big Shake-*down, *Special Agent, Mr. Moto's Last Warning, Rubber Racketeers, Mystery In Mexico, Bunco Squad, Party Girl.*

53 CRAWFORD, BRODERICK (1910–   ). U.S. actor, mainly heavy. More bully than tough guy, Crawford with careful casting could exude a melancholy menace that defied imitation. This quality encouraged Fellini to choose him to play the desperate con man in *Il Bidone/The Swindlers,* though his first choice had been Bogart. Best as the brutal husband in Lang's *Human Desire,* and the political boss in Rossen's *All The King's Men,* his Oscar-winner.

Films: *Little Miss Marker, Undercover*

Doctor, Slightly Honorable, Butch Minds the Baby, Broadway, Larceny Inc., Convicted, The Mob/Remember That Face, Scandal Sheet (1952)/*The Dark Page, Stop You're Killing Me, Down Three Dark Streets, New York Confidential, Big House U.S.A., Il Bidone/The Swindlers* (in Italy), *Convicts Four, A House Is Not a Home.*

54 CRICHTON, CHARLES (1910–). British director of prestigious first features in the Fifties but faded when faced with more ambitious projects: began *Birdman of Alcatraz,* but his material was scrapped and the film completed by Frankenheimer. Will be best remembered for the classic comedy *The Lavender Hill Mob,* and for *Law and Disorder,* comedy with Michael Redgrave as an unrepentant conman which Crichton finished after the death of Henry Cornelius.

Films: *The Lavender Hill Mob, Floods of Fear* (also wrote), *Law and Disorder.*

55 "CRIME DOES NOT PAY." Series of forty-eight M-G-M two-reel dramatised shorts which were a familiar part of programming in the late Thirties and Forties. As well as providing a training ground for promising young directors, some of whom later did well, it was a convenient testing place for European importations. "Your Crime Reporter" (Reed Hadley) introduced films on most types of crime from drug smuggling through espionage to faulty repairs on second-hand cars, although the political climate of the time sometimes led to excesses in which union leaders were depicted as seditious gangsters and many basic human rights viewed as less important than a well-ordered community. Familiar faces often appear; Robert Taylor, for instance, in *Buried*

Loot, first in the series and his first film role. 1935: *Buried Loot, Alibi Racket, Desert Death* (all George B. Seitz), *A Thrill for Thelma* (Edward L. Cahn). 1936: *Hit and Run Driver, Foolproof, Perfect Set-Up* (all Cahn), *The Public Pays* (Errol Taggart) (Academy Award). 1937: *Give Till It Hurts* (Felix Feist), *It May Happen to You, Soak the Poor, Torture Money* (Academy Award), *Behind the Criminal* (all Harold S. Bucquet). 1938: *A Criminal Is Born, Miracle Money* (both Leslie Fenton), *They're Always Caught, What Price Safety?* (both Bucquet), *Think It Over* (Jacques Tourneur), *The Wrong Way Out* (Gustav Machaty). 1939: *Drunk Driving* (David Miller), *Help Wanted, While America Sleeps* (both Fred Zinnemann), *Money To Loan* (Joe Newman), *Think First* (Roy Rowland), *Pound Foolish* (Feist). 1940: *Buyer Beware, Know Your Money, Women in Hiding* (all Newman), *Jack Pot, You the People* (both Rowland), *Soak the Old* (Sammy Lee). 1941: *Coffins on Wheels, Respect the Law, Don't Talk* (all Newman), *Forbidden Passage* (Zinnemann), *Sucker List* (Rowland). 1942: *For the Common Defence* (Allan R. Kenward), *Keep 'Em Sailing* (Basil Wrangell). 1944: *Dark Shadows* (Walter Hart), *Patrolling the Ether* (Paul Burnford). *Easy Life* (Hart). 1945: *A Gun in His Hand* (Joseph Losey), *Fall Guy* (Reg Le Borg), *The Last Installment* (Walter Hart), *Phantoms Inc.* (Harold Young), *Purity Squad* (Harold Kress). 1947: *Luckiest Guy in the World* (Newman).

56 CROMWELL, JOHN (1888–). Highly professional U.S. director whose crime films, though not typical of his work, have been accomplished. In *Algiers* he created a version of the Gabin *Pépé Le*

Opposite : Eleanor Parker in John Cromwell's CAGED

Moko (1937) that exceeded in part the original, and in *Caged* the most impressive of all "women in jail" films.

Films: *The Mighty, Street of Chance, For the Defence, Scandal Sheet* (1931), *The Vice Squad, Algiers, Caged, The Racket* (1951).

57 CURTIZ, MICHAEL (1888–1962). The most talented of all Warner Brothers' pre-war directors, and the Hollywood giant of the Forties. His films betray a ferocious talent, an impatience with irrelevancies wedded to a cynical and precise technique.

Films: *The Strange Love of Molly Louvain, 20,000 Years in Sing Sing, Private Detective 62, The Kennel Murder Case, Jimmy the Gent, The Case of the Curious Bride, Front Page Woman, Little Big Shot, Kid Galahad* (1937), *Angels with Dirty Faces, We're No Angels.*

58 DANTON, RAY (1931–). American actor, Fifties incarnation of George Raft, whom he played in *The George Raft Story/Spin of a Coin.* Quick, cool, almost a figure from the Thirties, he is generally miscast, though his "Legs" Diamond in Budd Boetticher's film and in *Portrait of a Mobster,* the biography of "Dutch" Schultz, is well judged.

James Cagney and Pat O'Brien at the climax of Curtiz's ANGELS WITH DIRTY FACES

Films: *Outside the Law, The Big Operator/Anatomy of the Syndicate, The Rise and Fall of Legs Diamond, Portrait of a Mobster, The George Raft Story/Spin of a Coin, F.B.I. Code 98.*

Above: Jules Dassin

Above: Ray Danton in THE RISE AND FALL OF LEGS DIAMOND

59 DASSIN, JULES (1911–   ). U.S. director, responsible for working out during the late Forties much of the mythology of the modern gangster film. With Mark Hellinger, for whom he directed *The Naked City* and *Brute Force,* he characterised the purest expression of socialist sentiment and humanism in the field. Leaving the U.S. in 1950 after the Communist witch-hunts—a scenarist on *The Naked City,* Albert Maltz, was also one of the Hollywood Ten—he created in Europe a distinguished career, and made in *Du Rififi Chez les Hommes/* (*Rififi* in U.K. and U.S.) the first and greatest of the "big job" gangster dramas.

Films: *Two Smart People, Brute Force, The Naked City, Thieves' Highway, Night*

and the City (in U.K.), *Du Rififi Chez les Hommes* (in France) (as "Perlo Vita" Dassin also played the traitor Cesar) *Topkapi* (in Turkey). Sequels to *Rififi* include *Rififi and the Women, Rififi in Panama* and Jacques Deray's excellent *Rififi in Tokyo.*

60 DAVIS, BETTE (1908–   ). Frail, delicate and game city girl in Warner's movies—the virgin moll of the Thirties. Davis's gangster movies are a footnote to her career, but they provide some subtle delights: a fugitive in *Bureau of Missing Persons* drawn out of hiding by her own funeral, secretary in *Parachute Jumper* lusted after by mobster Leo Carillo, a heroine bemused by an impenetrable script in Dieterle's *Maltese Falcon* re-make *Satan Met a Lady.* Silly in *The Petrified Forest,* pathetic as "Apple Annie" in Capra's *A Pocketful of Miracles,* she conveyed in her best films the core of resource and flip humour that is the city's sole legacy to its inhabitants.

Bette Davis with Allen Jenkins, George Brent, and Joseph Sawyer in SPECIAL AGENT

Films: *Hell's House, Three on a Match, 20,000 Years in Sing Sing, Parachute Jumper, Bureau of Missing Persons, The Big Shakedown, Jimmy the Gent, Fog over 'Frisco, Special Agent, The Petrified Forest, Satan Met a Lady, Marked Woman, Kid Galahad* (1937), *A Pocketful of Miracles*.

61 THE DEAD END KIDS. Bobby Jordan, Huntz Hall, Billy Halop, Leo Gorcey, Bernard Punsley, Gabriel Dell: child stars of Wyler's *Dead End* who proved so popular as Humphrey Bogart's juvenile auxiliary that they remained together for many years, changing their name as they grew older to the Bowery Boys.

Films: *Dead End, Crime School, They Made Me a Criminal, Hell's Kitchen, The Angels Wash Their Faces.*

62 DEARDEN, BASIL (1911–   ). English director who, often with producer/designer Michael Relph, has made films on many urban crime subjects, always with a lively sense of location and at least a superficial consciousness of contemporary social problems. Topics include complex robbery plans (*Cage of Gold*), juvenile delinquency (*The Blue Lamp, Violent Playground*), gentlemanly and comic robbery and extortion (*The League of Gentleman, Only When I Larf*), the race problem (*Sapphire*), homosexuality and blackmail (*Victim*), even the international thriller (*Masquerade*) and period romp (*The Assassination Bureau*). His best film is *The League of Gentlemen*, with a hand-picked team of cashiered army officers robbing a bank and reliving wartime escapades. The opening shot of Jack Hawkins emerging from a sewer grating in impeccable bowler and lounge suit is unforgettable.

63 DE CORSIA, TED (1906–   ).

American actor, always villain. He was Garza the fugitive in *The Naked City*, and the Murder Inc. organiser in *The Enforcer/Murder Inc.* who orders new recruit Zero Mostel "Get rid of that tent you're wearing and buy yourself a suit."

Films: *The Naked City, The Enforcer/ Murder Inc., Crime Wave/The City Is*

Dark, The Big Combo, The Steel Jungle, The Killing, Slightly Scarlet (1955), The Midnight Story/Appointment with a Shadow, Baby Face Nelson, The Joker Is Wild, Man on the Prowl, Inside the Mafia.

64 DELON, ALAIN (1935–   ).

French actor whose interest in the underworld has drawn him into some difficult situations and associations, but added also to his ability in gangster roles. His trench-coated ascetic gunman in *Le Samourai* is the quintessence of the type which Bogart and Ladd worked in vain to define.

Films: *Plein Soleil/Full Sun, Mélodie En Sous-Sol/The Big Snatch, Once a Thief* (in U.S.A.), *Les Félins/Joy House/ The Love Cage, Le Samourai, Le Clan des Siciliens, Borsalino.*

The Dead End Kids in ANGELS WITH DIRTY FACES

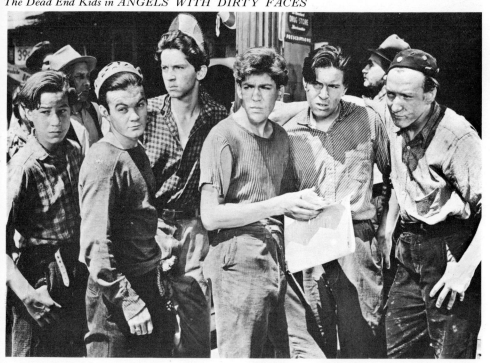

Ted De Corsia in Dassin's THE NAKED CITY

65 DEL RUTH, ROY (1895–1961). American director, another alumnus of Warner Brothers in the Thirties and skilled employer of Cagney, Robinson and Raft. His *The Maltese Falcon/ Dangerous Female* (1931) lacks the electric character conflict of Huston's version, but Ricardo Cortez as a slightly greasy Spade and Bebe Daniels as the heroine have their moments. It is a Thirties version of a Thirties story—Huston and hindsight have made it look more than the routine melodrama it is.

Films: *Blonde Crazy, The Maltese Falcon/Dangerous Female* (1931), *Taxi, The Little Giant, Bureau of Missing Persons, Lady Killer, Bulldog Drummond Strikes Back, It Had to Happen, Red Light, Stop You're Killing Me!* (re-make of *A Slight Case of Murder*).

66 DEXTER, BRAD (1922–   ). American actor, lately producer (*The Naked Runner*). Too decent looking to be a good heavy, Dexter seems born to have his head blown off. His crooked private eye in *The Asphalt Jungle* is a piece of nice casting by Huston.

Films: *The Asphalt Jungle, The Las Vegas Story, Macao, 99 River Street, Violent Saturday, House of Bamboo, Johnny Cool.*

67 DIETERLE, WILLIAM (1893–   ). German director, formerly actor, one of the many polished artists Warners

46

Alain Delon slaps Ann-Margret in ONCE A THIEF

turned out in the Thirties.

Films: *Jewel Robbery, Man Wanted, Lawyer Man, From Headquarters, Fog over 'Frisco, Satan Met a Lady, Dark City, The Accused, The Turning Point.*

68 DILLINGER, JOHN (1903–1934).

"You know what Dillinger said about himself, and people like you," the gang boss says to Bogart's Roy Earle in *High Sierra.* "You're rushing towards death, just rushing towards death." The rush ended on the pavement in front of the Biograph Theatre, 2433 Lincoln Avenue, Chicago, on July 22, 1934, when Dillinger, betrayed by one of the women with whom he liked to surround himself, was shot down from ambush by the F.B.I.

The film he had just seen, *Manhattan Melodrama,* was a Woody Van Dyke crime drama.

He looked like Bogart and shared his thin-lipped smile. When Chicago F.B.I. chief Melvin H. Purvis, killer of most of the rural bandits, examined the body of his victim, he found that Dillinger had undergone crude plastic surgery, the scars of his bullet wounds erased, his nose altered and his fingerprints mutilated with acid. But even the most complete re-making could not have saved Dillinger. From the beginning of his brief criminal career he was marked, he knew, to die.

Among the bandits of his period, Dillinger (pronounced with a hard "g," as in "finger") stood out as a criminal of style and intelligence. His hauls in 1933/1934 came to more than $250,000, and one, from the robbery of the bank at Greencastle, Ind., netted $144,000, probably a record for the time. Yet he was not a murderer, seldom had need to fire his gun, and it is doubtful whether he ever killed a man, even another bandit. He is credited with introducing to crime the machine gun, bullet-proof vests, cutting torches for safecracking and fast-car getaways, questionable claims but indicative of the respect in which he was held by police and public.

Critics of the F.B.I. have tried to minimise Dillinger's exploits and therefore the feat of trapping him, but the legend seems solidly rooted in fact. His robberies mark Dillinger as brave, resourceful and intelligent. Imprisoned in the allegedly escape-proof jail at Crown Point, Ind., in March 1934 he bluffed his way out with a fake gun despite a massive cordon of police and National Guardsmen. Later claims that the gun was genuine, smuggled in by a corrupt judge, merely add to the story; real or false, it was never discharged. Even the New York *Times* of July 23, 1934, admitted respectfully that the Crown Point escapade "made him an international figure of legendary proportions." And it is typical of both Dillinger and the American people that he should, in the middle of the national manhunt that followed his escape, visit his father in Mooresville, Ind., and that the neighbours, moved by his filial devotion, should have petitioned for his pardon.

In 1933 Will Hays of the Production Code Authority forbade any film on Dillinger, but *Public Hero No. 1* (1935), while glorifying the G-Man, had a theatre gunfight recalling Dillinger's death. *False Faces/Let 'Em Have It* (1935)

and *Undercover Doctor* (1939) both dealt with plastic surgery on fugitive criminals. Many films on the Thirties bandits refer to Dillinger briefly, stressing mainly his death outside a cinema, a grisly parable of the relationship between film fantasy and fact that audiences particularly relish.

High Sierra (1941), based on Dillinger but not following his life precisely, is the finest retelling of the legend. Bogart conveys much of it; Dillinger's romanticism—released from jail, he goes straight to a park and walks among the trees; his sexuality, devoted to a fragile and touching Ida Lupino; and the habits of a country boy, shown in his help to bumpkin Henry Travers and his club-footed grand-daughter. The John Huston/W. R. Burnett script does not minimise the violence, the callous shootings or the final gun-battle, but they are integrated into the pattern of Earle's behaviour, contrasted with the viciousness of those who hunt him. Looking around at the people gathered at the foot of the mountain on which Earle is cornered, a radio reporter says, "In the light of the flares, their faces are like the faces of the dead. Everything is dead, except their eyes."

The re-make of *High Sierra* (*I Died a Thousand Times,* 1955) conveys only a shadow of the original, as does *Dillinger* (1945) with Lawrence Tierney, and *Young Dillinger* (1964), with Nick Adams, unsure as to whether Dillinger was a cold-eyed killer or a mixed-up kid who fought to save his pregnant teenage wife. In *Baby Face Nelson,* the relationship between Dillinger (Leo Gordon) and the insane trigger-happy Nelson, who was briefly in his gang, opens some intriguing areas of speculation, but the matter is dropped in favour of more gratuitous violence.

Of the F.B.I.'s part in the killing of

Dillinger, *The F.B.I. Story* shows a sanitised version only, omitting the technical illegality of the raid—Dillinger's only federal offence was to drive a stolen car across a state line, hardly enough to shoot him for—and its comic opera aspects—worried by the infiltration of his theatre by sixteen hard-eyed armed men, the manager called Chicago city police, to whom Purvis was forced to explain his high-handed and unauthorised raid into their territory.
Also *Guns Don't Argue*.

69 DMYTRYK, EDWARD (1908–).
American director, creator in *Murder My Sweet/Farewell My Lovely* of Hollywood's best Raymond Chandler adaptation.
Films: *Emergency Squad, Secrets of the Lone Wolf, Confessions of Boston Blackie, Seven Miles from Alcatraz, The Falcon Strikes Back, Murder My Sweet/Farewell My Lovely, Cornered, Crossfire, The Sniper*.

70 DONLEVY, BRIAN (1899–).
Poker-faced and soft-spoken U.S. actor who conveys a quality of sincerity sometimes well used by gangster film directors.
Films: *36 Hours To Kill, Midnight Taxi, Behind Prison Gates, Human Cargo, The Glass Key* (1943), *Kiss of Death, The Lucky Stiff, Shakedown, Hoodlum Empire, The Big Combo, A Cry in the Night*.

71 DOUGLAS, GORDON (1910–).
Competent U.S. director who has been successful at Westerns, science fiction and gangster films. His best is *Kiss Tomorrow Goodbye*, starring and produced by Cagney, but lately he has combined with Frank Sinatra to make a variety of interesting crime films, both comic and serious.
Films: *The Falcon in Hollywood, San Quentin* (1946), *Kiss Tomorrow Goodbye, Between Midnight and Dawn/Prowl Car, The Fiend Who Walked the West* (Western re-make of *Kiss of Death*), *Robin and the Seven Hoods, Tony Rome, Lady in Cement, The Detective*.

72 DURYEA, DAN (1907–1969). U.S.
actor, usually sneering thug, sadistic and brutal, though often with a morbid sense of humour. His Silky in *Larceny* (1948) under George Sherman's direction is a brilliant cameo of murderous cunning.
Films: *Ball of Fire, Main Street after Dark, Black Angel, Larceny, Johnny Stool Pigeon, Manhandled, Criss Cross, Too Late for Tears, One Way Street, Chicago Calling, The Burglar, Slaughter on Tenth Avenue, Platinum High School/Rich Young & Deadly*.

73 EGAN, RICHARD (1921–   ). American leading man of the Fifties, his trademark a fixed toothy snarl.

Films: *Highway 301, Undercover Girl, The Damned Don't Cry, The Killer That Stalked New York/The Frightened City, Split Second, Violent Saturday, Slaughter on Tenth Avenue.*

74 FARRELL, GLENDA (1904–   ). Lively American character actress, usually a wise-cracking assistant or frank young sister. Shared the "Torchy Blane" series with Jane Wyman and others in the late Thirties playing a girl reporter always in trouble.

Films: *Little Caesar, I Am a Fugitive from a Chain Gang, Three on a Match, Bureau of Missing Persons, The Big Shakedown, Little Big Shot, Lady for a Day, Torchy Blane in Chinatown, Prison Break, Torchy Gets Her Man, Torchy Runs for Mayor, Johnny Eager, A Night for Crime, I Love Trouble.*

75 FARROW, JOHN (1904–1963). Skilful Australian-born director who learned at RKO in the Fifties how to show Mitchum's feline power and Glenn Ford's stiff-chinned resolve. *Plunder of the Sun,* an "Aztec Falcon" with Ford the numbed hero, Patricia Medina the ambiguous heroine and Francis L. Sullivan the white-clad "fat man" is good fun.

Films: original story: *The Bad One.* As director: *Full Confession, The Saint Strikes Back, Code of the Streets, The Big Clock, Red Hot and Blue, Alias Nick Beal, Plunder of the Sun, His Kind of Woman, A Bullet Is Waiting.*

76 F.B.I. (Federal Bureau of Investigation). The U.S. Federal Government's law enforcement arm, run since 1924 by J. Edgar Hoover and reflecting his small-town morality and personal ambition. Originally established by Theodore Roosevelt in 1908 to police mail, tax and public land abuses, the F.B.I. was occupied in its early years with preventing minor crimes like smuggling contraceptives, obscene books and prize-fight films across state lines. In 1910, the Mann Act, forbidding transport of women between states for immoral purposes, gave it the beginning of real power.

The real boost came in 1934 when, after the Lindbergh kidnap case, Congress made kidnapping a Federal offence punishable by death, and to the list of Federal crimes added robbing a national bank, flight of a defendant across state lines to avoid prosecution or giving testimony, the transmission of threats by any means whatsoever, racketeering practices by businessmen engaged in interstate commerce, transporting stolen property across a state line and resisting a Federal officer.

Hoover took this as a mandate to fight all crime and moved in (often without State consultation) on the rural bandits still at large. His Chicago man, Melvin H. Purvis, tracked down John Dillinger and Charles "Pretty Boy" Floyd, while others engineered the deaths of "Ma" Barker, "Baby Face" Nelson and others, and Capone's arrest on minor charges, giving the tax authorities time to investigate his records. The myth of the G-man, incorruptible hammer of the hoodlum, was carefully fostered by Hoover and his staff, but the organisation made little impression on the hard core of criminal power.

During the Second World War, the F.B.I. chose to concentrate on abuses of national security, and in doing this ignored such organisations as "Murder Inc," until public pressure forced them to intervene. Generally, however, it is through cases like the arrest of Hiss and

Lee Marvin and Ernest Borgnine in VIOLENT SATURDAY

the Rosenbergs that we remember the modern F.B.I., and their gangbusting activities are part of the past.

Films have not been slow to reflect the F.B.I.'s rise. *G-Men* (1935) sold the Hoover line, with Cagney as an incorruptible opponent of the gangsters. Most films on Floyd, Dillinger, and Bonnie and Clyde included tributes to the organisation, and to its combination of training, science and courage. *Held For Ransom* (1938) and *F.B.I. Girl* (1951) dealt with G-women, and the "Junior G-Man" serials with their juvenile auxiliary. *The House on 92nd St.* was Henry Hathaway's documentary reconstruction of F.B.I. action against German spies during the war, one of many. *The F.B.I. Story* (1959), though purporting to be the real truth, merely showed James Stewart and his men as puppets operating under Hoover's all-seeing eye.

See also G-MEN, JOHN DILLINGER, CHARLES "PRETTY BOY" FLOYD, MURDER INC.

77 FLEISCHER, RICHARD (1916–). Talented U.S. director, similar in style to Aldrich but not accorded his opportunities. His *The Narrow Margin* is one of the most gripping of Hollywood thrillers.

Films: *Bodyguard, Follow Me Quietly,*

Trapped, Armored Car Robbery, The Narrow Margin, Violent Saturday, The Boston Strangler.

78 FLEMING, RHONDA (1923–).
Fetching red-head, leading lady in some Fifties dramas. She ventilates Ted de Corsia with a spear-gun at the end of Dwan's *Slightly Scarlet*.

Films: *Out of the Past/Build My Gallows High, Cry Danger, While the City Sleeps, Slightly Scarlet* (1956).

79 FLOREY, ROBERT (1900–).
French-born director who has worked mostly in Hollywood, lately exclusively in TV. In the late Thirties he made a series of bizarre crime melodramas with Akim Tamiroff at Paramount.

Films: *The Hole in the Wall, I Am a Thief, King of Gamblers, King of Alcatraz, Dangerous To Know, Parole Fixer, Meet Boston Blackie, Lady Gangster, Roger Touhy Gangster/The Last Gangster, The Crooked Way, Johnny One-Eye, The Vicious Years.*

80 FLOYD, CHARLES ARTHUR ("Pretty Boy") (– 1934).
In the fast company of Dillinger and Kelly, Charles Floyd was a minor character. His robberies were small, his most notorious activities created largely out of speculation and myth. Even the newspapers recognised the phenomenon. In October, 1934, the New York *Times* wrote, "Visitors to the Southwest brought back stories of his prowess that strongly hinted that fact and fiction had begun to merge. But," it added quickly, "It was established that he was fearless and a good shot, an amazingly skilful automobile driver, a killer and a man with a quaint pride in the fact that his robbery victims were generally rich."

It was this aspect of the legend about which Woody Guthrie wrote his famous folk song, painting him as a rural man of honour forced into crime by police brutality and kept there by a public that attributed to him every unsolved robbery. He almost certainly did rob an Akron, Ohio bank in 1930, and kill a policeman in his escape, but the string of alleged Floyd crimes in Indiana, Missouri and Arkansas would have taxed an army. By late 1933 Floyd was the focus of unprecedented national hysteria, one entire New York suburb was thrown into terror by the appearance on the street of a car with Oklahoma plates.

To his death, Floyd denied any complicity in the worst crime laid to his name, the so-called Kansas City Massacre of June 19, 1933, in which three men with machine guns ambushed a car in front of the Kansas City Union Station and methodically riddled the vehicle and five of its six passengers, including bank robber Frank Nash and his F.B.I. and state guards. Gangster Vern Miller was later accused of the murders, and his companions identified as Floyd and his regular partner Adam Richetti. The sources of this information were never revealed, and Floyd denied all complicity, even when dying of wounds.

Using the Kansas City Massacre as grounds for a federal hunt, Melvin Purvis, killer of Dillinger, set out after Floyd, and finally tracked him down at a farm outside East Liverpool, Ohio, on October 22, 1934. Although Guthrie's song told of how Floyd was loved by the poor, it was a farmhand who betrayed him to the police while he begged another to help him escape. Fleeing across the fields, he was cut down by machine gun fire. As for the story that he committed his first crime, the assault of a deputy sheriff, because the man used bad language in his wife's hearing, it seems contradictory that Ruby Floyd, his estranged wife, supported herself after his death by lecturing on "Crime Does Not Pay" throughout the Midwest.

Floyd was buried at Akins, Okla., in a plot he had chosen for himself in May 1933. Until his death his mother tended it carefully, knowing, like her son, that it would not be long before it was filled. A halting attempt was made at his life story by Herbert J. Leder in 1959, with an excessively handsome John Ericson as Floyd. Not especially "Pretty," Floyd earned his nickname from a nervous tendency to comb his well-oiled hair, but in *Pretty Boy Floyd* Ericson is a narcissistic killer lacking both Guthrie's folkhero charisma and the real Floyd's resilience and skill.

81 FORD, GLENN (1916–).

Servicable leading man of U.S. thrillers in the Forties and Fifties.

Films: *My Son Is Guilty, Convicted Woman, Framed, The Undercover Man, Convicted, Plunder of the Sun, The Big Heat, The Blackboard Jungle, The Money Trap.*

82 FORD, JOHN (1895–).

Though not among his best, Ford's crime films have a characteristic energy and strong comic qualities. His *The Whole Town's Talking*, with Edward G. Robinson as a mild clerk mistaken for the gang boss he resembles, is classic.

Films: *The Girl in No. 29, The Big Punch, Riley The Cop, Born Reckless, Up the River* (1930), *The Whole Town's Talking, Gideon's Day/Gideon of Scotland Yard* (in U.K.).

83 FOSTER, PRESTON (1902–).

Reliable Thirties leading man at Warners who unsuccessfully battled his spare tyre through the Forties as an overweight private eye in films like *The Bermuda Mystery*. Moderately convincing as Roger Touhy in Florey's biopic, and as a gang leader in *Kansas City Confidential*.

Films: *I Am a Fugitive from a Chain Gang, The Last Mile* (1932), *Two Seconds, Wharf Angel, Muss 'Em Up, Lady in the Morgue, The Last Warning, Up the River* (1938), *Night in New Orleans, Inside Job, Roger Touhy Gangster/The Last Gangster, Kansas City Confidential, I The Jury, The Secret Four.*

84 FULLER, SAMUEL (1916–).

American director. If you are tired of Sam Fuller you are tired of movies. It's fair to paraphrase Johnson because this is Johnsonian cinema, anecdotal, irascible, journalistic. Pulp novelist, newsman and screenwriter Fuller has given screen violence much of its grammar; the sprawl of struck men through breakable objects to accentuate their fall is just one new trick. In subjects, Fuller is Grub Street;

cheap exposés, bizarre plots, exotic locales are his specialties. But almost always he transcends yellow journalism to expose the rotten core of urban life and the hangover mouth of the urban wolf.

Films: original story: *Gangs of New York, Federal Man Hunt, Bowery Boy, Gangs of the Waterfront, Scandal Sheet/ The Dark Page*. As screenwriter: *Shockproof* (with Helen Deutsch). As director: *Pick-Up on South Street, House of Bamboo, The Crimson Kimono, Underworld U.S.A.*

85   GABIN, JEAN (1904–   ). Gabin's combination of tough professional and man of feelings has been used often in plots where, as the top pro., he is drawn into disaster by sentiment or sex. As Max Le Menteur, fiftyish criminal mastermind in Becker's *Touchez Pas au Grisbi,* he said it all in a masterful performance. "I have put many kinds of people on film in my time, but never anyone so photogenic. He is a cinematic force."—Jean Renoir.

Films: *L'Etoile de Valencia, Pépé le Moko* (1937), *Miroir, Touchez Pas au Grisbi, Razzia sur la Chnouf, Gas-Oil, Le Rouge Est Mis, Le Désordré et la Nuit, Maigret Tend un Piège, Maigret et l'Affaire Saint Fiacre, Le Cave Se Rebiffe, Mélodie en Sous-Sol/The Big Snatch, Le Pacha, Le Clan des Siciliens.*

86   GABLE, CLARK (1901–1960). Back in the early days of sound at Metro, Gable was a newsman crusading against vice in *The Secret Six,* a gangster in *A Free Soul* and *The Finger Points* and the alter ego to William Powell, executed in the last reel of *Manhattan Melodrama.* Much later, in *Any Number Can Play* (1949), he was a smooth gambler fighting off a variety of threats.

87   GARFIELD, JOHN (1913–1952). Rugged U.S. leading man whose choice of roles—maltreated and bitter delinquent, duped boxer, honourable gangster —reflected his strong socialist views. At his best as the young tough in *Dust Be My Destiny* fighting to stop a slide into crime brought on by social injustice.

Films: *They Made Me a Criminal, Dust Be My Destiny, Castle on the Hudson, East of the River, Out of the Fog, Body and Soul, Force of Evil, He Ran All the Way.*

88   GARLAND, BEVERLEY (1926–   ). Strong-featured and polished U.S. actress able to suggest both menace and fortitude.

Films: *D.O.A., The Miami Story, New*

Opposite page : Cliff Robertson with Robert Emhardt in Fuller's UNDERWORLD U.S.A. At left : Jean Gabin

Above : Clark Gable with Wallace Beery, Jean Harlow and Lewis Stone (seated) in THE SECRET SIX. At left : John Garfield

Orleans Uncensored, The Desperate Hours, Riot On Pier 6, The Steel Jungle, Chicago Confidential, Chicago Deadline, Swamp Women, The Joker Is Wild.

Also TV series *Decoy* as policewoman.

89 GARMES, LEE (1898–   ). Brilliant U.S. cinematographer, sometime director/producer, associated for many years with Ben Hecht.

Films : *City Streets, Scarface, Angels Over Broadway, The Secret Life of Walter*

Mitty, Detective Story, The Captive City, The Desperate Hours, Never Love a Stranger.

90 G-MEN. Government men, i.e. F.B.I. agents. A description allegedly used first by George "Machine Gun" Kelly on his arrest in 1934, but probably coined by Hoover as part of his Thirties advertising campaign for the Bureau. Title of Warner's 1935 film, and used in many others, e.g. *Trapped by G-Men* (Lewis Collins, 1937), *Border G-Man* (David Howard, 1938), *When G-Men Step In* (C. C. Coleman, 1938) etc. Also serials *Junior G-Men* (1940), *Junior G-Men of the Air* (1942), *G-Men Never Forget* (1947) etc. *See also* F.B.I., T-MEN.

91 GOMEZ, THOMAS (1905–). Fat American actor, expert in roles as corrupt cop, minor crook. Excellent as the fearful operator of the "numbers racket" in *Force of Evil*.

Films: *The Dark Mirror, Ride the Pink Horse, Key Largo, Force of Evil, Sorrowful Jones, The Sellout, Macao, Las Vegas Shakedown.*

92 GOODIS, DAVID (1917–1967). American novelist whose works, though few, have been the source of some important films, a fact not grasped until

Gary Cooper in CITY STREETS, photographed by Lee Garmes

"*I'll be waiting for you when you come out....*" 1310-12

Truffaut used one of them, *Down There,* as the basis of *Tirez Sur le Pianiste/Don't Shoot the Pianist.* Original story: *Dark Passage* (script by Delmer Daves), *Nightfall* (script by Stirling Silliphant). As screenwriter: *The Burglar.*

93 GRAHAME, GLORIA (1925–). A tiny mouth, big eyes and the sulky sexy look that gangster heroines need have still failed to give this actress the opportunities she deserves. Although her best roles — *The Bad and the Beautiful, Human Desire* — have been non-crime films, she will go down in history as the lady scalded with hot coffee by Lee Marvin in Lang's *The Big Heat.*

Films: *Crossfire, Song of the Thin Man, Macao, The Big Heat, Naked Alibi, The Good Die Young, Odds against Tomorrow.*

94 GRINDE, NICK (1894–). One of the cleverest U.S. directors of crime and horror films in the Thirties and Forties, with a style and pace greater than his contemporaries.

Films: *The Bishop Murder Case, Public Enemy's Wife/G-Man's Wife, Jailbreak, Sudden Money, Federal Manhunt, Convicted Woman, King of Chinatown, The Road to Alcatraz.*

95 GUFFEY, BURNETT (1905–). Guffey's cinematographic career reaches from the Thirties to the present day, but his eye for the reality of urban life has never dimmed. Not one of the major cameramen of the golden age, he is nevertheless a talent of interest.

Films: *Johnny O'Clock, Knock on Any Door, The Undercover Man, Convicted, Scandal Sheet/The Dark Page* (1952), *The Sniper, Private Hell 36, Tight Spot, The Brothers Rico, Edge of Eternity, The True Story of Lynne Stuart, Nightfall, Let No Man Write My Epitaph, Birdman of Alcatraz, Bonnie and Clyde, The Split.*

96 HAMMETT, DASHIELL (1894–1961). It is astonishing that Hammett, who had more influence on the field of detective fiction than any man before Chandler, should have written only five novels and that only three of these should have been filmed. *The Maltese Falcon* (1930) has had three incarnations; under its own name in 1931, directed by Roy Del Ruth, in 1941, directed by John Huston. In 1936 as *Satan Met a Lady* it provided some laughs and endless confusion to both audience and cast of Bette Davis and Warren William.

Frank Tuttle shot *The Glass Key* (1931) in 1935, and Stuart Heisler in 1942. *The Thin Man* (1932), clearly a pot-boiler, has had a longer life than any, being the basis of Metro's successful series with William Powell and Myrna Loy. Hammett's first two books, *Red Harvest* and *The Dain Curse* (both 1929) have never been filmed, an unaccountable error, considering their crisp dialogue and intriguing plots. All that remains of him from this period is some memorably realistic material in his script for Rouben Mamoulian's *City Streets* (1931).

Hammett's personal history is appropriately bizarre. For eight years he

Donald Sutherland, Ernest Borgnine, Jim Brown, Warren Oates, and Julie Harris in THE SPLIT, photographed by Burnett Guffey

Bette Davis and Warren William in SATAN MET A LADY, inspired by Dashiell Hammett

was a Pinkerton detective, working on, among others, the "Fatty" Arbuckle case and on the arrest of gambler Nick Arnstein, basis of the film *Funny Girl*. Strongly Leftist, Hammett was jailed in 1951 for six months for failing to reveal the source of funds he held as trustee of the Civil Rights Congress, information which he probably did not possess. In his combination of progressive political views, mordant sense of style and clear-eyed appraisal of the urban world, he was the essential artist of the *genre* he created.

97 HARLOW, JEAN (1911–1937). Odd that Harlow, symbol of eroticism and forbidden sex, should have made only four gangster films, and been an outright "bad girl" in none of them. It probably proves that the Harlow *persona,* like that of most Metro heroines of the Thirties, was restricted to a handful of values, with resource, flip humour and taunting but unattainable sex at their head. But it was still enough to make Cagney push a grapefruit in Mae Clark's face in *The Public Enemy* and go in pursuit of her.

Films: *The Secret Six, The Public Enemy, The Beast of the City, Hold Your Man.*

98 HATHAWAY, HENRY (1898–). Veteran American director, one of the most relentless artists of the post-war period. The streak of documentary realism in his films makes them entertainments that remain indelibly in the mind.

Films: *Johnny Apollo, The House on 92nd Street, The Dark Corner, Kiss of Death, Call Northside 777, 23 Paces to Baker Street, Seven Thieves.*

99 HAWKS, HOWARD (1896–   ).

Like most of the great American directors, Hawks is master of any *genre* to which he turns his hand. His gangster films, though few, are seminal: *The Criminal Code,* a chilling picture of prison life, its rules of honour and shifting allegiances; *Scarface,* the essential Capone parallel, marred only by moral strictures that turn his Borgia-like Tony Camonte from a raving beast at the climax to a penitent and quivering shell; *Ball of Fire,* classic comedy of gangsterdom face to face with innocence in the form of seven don dwarves compiling an encyclopedia (this was re-made, unsuccessfully, by Hawks as *A Song Is Born*); perhaps finest of all *The Big Sleep,* less a reading of Chandler than a tribute to the potency of the Bogart/Bacall partnership. Of the last, scenarist Leigh Brackett recalls the worthlessness of William Faulkner's dialogue, Bogart's ad-libbing of many fine scenes, but most the electricity of the stars, then newly married and working in complete accord.

100 HAYDEN, STERLING (1916–   ).

An unlikely gangster hero, Hayden's sulky look, sullen stance and country-boy voice nevertheless exert a strange appeal. Able to suggest corruption in an essentially honest man, he explored this role in *The Asphalt Jungle* and *The Killing.*

Films: *Manhandled, The Asphalt Jungle, Crime Wave/The City Is Dark, Naked Alibi, Suddenly, Five Steps to Danger, The Come-On, The Killing, Hard Contract.*

101 HECHT, BEN (1894–1964).

American screen-writer, ex-newsman and playwright, occasional novelist, short story writer and producer/director. Difficult to work with, his films were almost always collaborations, usually with equals like Charles Lederer, sometimes with pupils. All retain, however, a strain of Hecht's socialist/humanist ethic and clinical eye for detail in dialogue.

Films: *Underworld* (Academy Award), *Scarface* (with Seton I. Miller, John Lee Mahin, W. R. Burnett), *Angels over Broadway* (wrote, produced and directed), *Ride the Pink Horse* (with Charles Lederer), *Kiss of Death* (with Charles Lederer), *Where the Sidewalk Ends.* (*Ride the Pink Horse* was re-made as *The Hanged Man* and *Kiss of Death* as *The Fiend Who Walked the West.*)

102 HEISLER, STUART (1894–   ).

U.S. editor who directed two gangster re-makes—*The Glass Key* (1943) from Frank Tuttle's 1935 classic, and *I Died a Thousand Times* (1955) from Walsh's *High Sierra* (1941).

103 HELLINGER, MARK (1903–1947).

American newsman and columnist who, after a brief career in scriptwriting, became the most important of all Forties crime-film producers. His films are all journalistic in impact, strongly humanist in content.

Films: as scriptwriter: *Night Court, The Roaring Twenties* (story only). As producer: *It All Came True, Brother*

Over page: Sterling Hayden (tallest) with Elisha Cook Jr., Ted De Corsia and Marie Windsor in THE KILLING

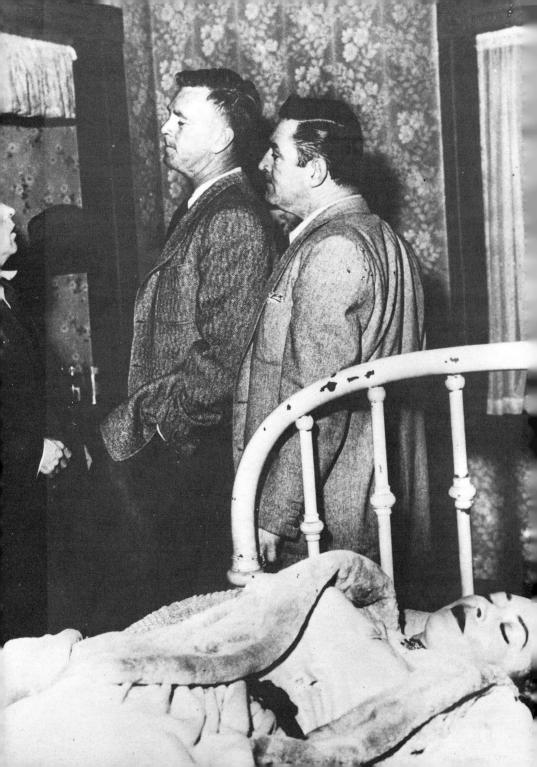

Mark Hellinger in 1947 with stars Ella Raines, Ann Blyth, Yvonne de Carlo and Anita Calby

Orchid, They Drive By Night, High Sierra, The Killers (1946), *Brute Force, The Naked City.*

104 HILL, GEORGE (1895–1934). Precise realist U.S. Twenties and Thirties director, former cameraman, who with wife and top screenwriter Frances Marion made one of M-G-M's best teams. Late in 1934 he killed himself, but not before he made two notable gangster films: *The Big House* (1930), first of the great prison films and probably the grimmest, and *The Secret Six* (1931), a thinly disguised Capone parallel

and a brutal picture of prohibition's corruption.

105 HOSSEIN, ROBERT. French leading man, often director/writer of his own films, which cast him in roles as brutal gang-leader or sinister menace.

Films: as actor: *Quai des Blondes, Du Rififi Chez les Hommes/Rififi, Série Noire, Les Salauds Vont en Enfer* (also original story and direction), *Méfiez-Vous Fillettes, Du Rififi Chez les Femmes/Rififi and the Women, Le Goût de la Violence* (original story and direction), *Le Jeu de la Vérité* (original story, script and

63

direction), *Le Meurtrier, Le Temps des Loups*.

106 HOWARD, TREVOR (1916–). English actor, reliable stand-by as detective or occasional heavy in thrillers of the late Forties and Fifties.

Films: *They Made Me a Fugitive, Green for Danger, The Golden Salamander, Interpol, Moment of Danger*.

107 HOWE, JAMES WONG (1899–). U.S. cameraman whose talent for contrasty monochrome photography has seldom been used effectively in crime films; exceptions are *The Criminal Code, Manhattan Melodrama, The Thin Man, Whipsaw, They Made Me a Criminal, He Ran All The Way*.

108 HUGHES, HOWARD (1905–). Mystery billionaire industrialist, inventor and sometime film producer. His credit on a handful of films probably indicates only that when they were made he had titular control of the studio, viz. his RKO productions of the early Fifties. But with Hughes one never knows—he did direct *Hell's Angels* and *The Outlaw*, with phenomenal results.

Films: as producer: *The Racket* (1928), *Scarface, The Racket* (1951), *His Kind of Woman, Macao*.

109 HUGHES, KEN (1922–). Memories of a clever little convict comedy with James Booth and Anthony Newley called *In the Nick* and his strained but ingenious reworking of *Macbeth* as a gangster film with Paul Douglas justify Hughes's inclusion. With Hollywood facilities he could have become a Seiler-like crime specialist, but Britain lacks the rich techniques that might have made this possible.

Films: *Wide Boy, Little Red Monkey, Joe Macbeth, The Long Haul, In the Nick, The Small World of Sammy Lee/The Small Violent World of Sammy Lee*.

110 HUSTON, JOHN (1906–). "Most of the really good popular art produced anywhere comes from Hollywood, and much of it bears (John) Huston's name." (James Agee, 1950.) Although he declined in later years to an uneven creator of misconceived if often arresting films, Huston's genius as a chronicler of the urban underworld will probably never be surpassed. At a time when to treat crime as anything more than a social disease was unthinkable, he got under the skin of thieves and gangsters to show the complex structure of their world and the painful moral necessities of their code.

"Crime is only a left-handed form of human endeavour," the weary, intelligent but corrupt attorney Louis Calhern says in *The Asphalt Jungle*, probably Huston's finest crime film. This theme, the duties of crime and the urban wolf's moral code, is a characteristic one. It has led him in his scripts and those films he directed to create a gallery of complex criminals, driven by motives of ominous moral necessity, or by forces far nobler than simple greed: Edward G. Robinson's Dr. Clitterhouse, whose scientific curiosity makes him a master criminal, vengeful Sam Spade in *The Maltese Falcon*, ignoring love in favour of a ritual expiation of his lover's sin, the inhabitants of *The Asphalt Jungle*, cops and criminals united in their contempt for the unprofessional, the weak, and, most

Opposite: Marie Prevost and Thomas Meighan in THE RACKET, produced in 1928 by Howard Hughes

moving, Bogart's Dillinger carbon Roy Earle in *High Sierra,* submitting with samurai resignation to the inevitability of violent death.

Films: As scriptwriter: *The Amazing Dr. Clitterhouse* (with John Wexley), *High Sierra* (with W. R. Burnett). As director: *The Maltese Falcon, Key Largo, The Asphalt Jungle* (also part script), *Beat the Devil.*

111 HUSTON, WALTER (1884–1950). Solid U.S. character actor, father of John Huston, usually cast as judge, politician, family man or person of dignity. Early in the Thirties he was roped in to play similar roles in crime pictures, usually with professionalism but little enthusiasm. He is still commanding as the warden in Hawks's *The Criminal Code* and crusading police chief in *The Beast of the City.*

Films: *The Criminal Code, The Star Witness, The Beast of the City, The Wet Parade, The Ruling Voice.*

112 JENKINS, ALLEN (1900–   ). American character actor, probably the most familiar of gangster faces. The basic ratty henchman, snap-brim hat, gun in pocket, fag in mouth and all, he is absent from few of the Warner Brothers crime classics of the Thirties and Forties.

Films: *I Am a Fugitive from a Chain Gang, Lawyer Man, Bureau of Missing Persons, The Mayor of Hell, The Big Shakedown, Jimmy the Gent, The Case of the Howling Dog, The Case of the Curious Bride, The Case of the Lucky Legs, Special Agent, Marked Woman, Dead End, Racket Busters, The Amazing Dr. Clitterhouse, Torchy Plays with Dynamite, Brother Orchid, The Gay Falcon, A Date with the Falcon, Eyes in the Night, Robin and the 7 Hoods.*

113 JONES, CAROLYN (1929–   ). Minor American actress with some good roles to her credit; was "Baby Face" Nelson's girl in Siegel's violent biopic.

Films: *The Turning Point, The Big Heat, Shield for Murder, Baby Face Nelson, Sail a Crooked Ship, Colour Me Dead* (in Australia).

114 KARLOFF, BORIS (1887–1969). With his tall but stooped body, hooded eyes and chillingly precise movements, Karloff made a splendid heavy, contributing some great portraits to crime film: murderous trusty Ned Galloway in *The Criminal Code* and mobster Gaffney in *Scarface.* He was less successful as Chinese detective Mr. Wong in a series of Monogram quickies 1938–1940.

Films: *The Bad One, The Criminal Code, Smart Money, The Guilty Generation, The Public Defender, Scarface, The Miracle Man, Behind the Mask, Mr. Wong Detective, The Mystery of Mr. Wong, Mr. Wong in Chinatown, The Fatal Hour, Doomed To Die* (last two also "Mr. Wong" series), *The Secret Life of Walter Mitty, Dick Tracy Meets Gruesome, Lured, Colonel March Investigates* (in U.K.).

115 KARLSON, PHIL (1908–   ). American director of well-paced gangster and crime films, a Monogram graduate who began on "Charlie Chan" thrillers and went on to do documentary-style *Five against the House,* about a Las Vegas casino robbery, one of the earliest "big caper" films, and *The Phenix City Story,* an uncompromising story of one man's attempt to clean up a corrupt southern city despite official inertia and public disinterest. Buffs prefer *The Shanghai Cobra,* 1945 "Charlie Chan" where the villain is a poisoned juke box, or *Wife Wanted* (1946), where ageing star

*James Cagney and Robert Armstrong
in G-MEN, directed by William Keighley*

Kay Francis (who co-produced) exposes a fake lonely hearts racket.

Films: *The Shanghai Cobra, Dark Alibi, Wife Wanted, Scandal Sheet* (1952)/*The Dark Page, Kansas City Confidential, 99 River St., Tight Spot, Five against the House, The Phenix City Story, The Brothers Rico, Kid Galahad* (1962), *The Scarface Mob.*

116 KEIGHLEY, WILLIAM (1889–). Journeyman Warner's director of the Thirties and Forties whose reputation as a gangster expert is based on the relatively routine *G-Men* and *Bullets or Ballots.*

Films: *Journal of a Crime, G-Men, Special Agent, Bullets or Ballots, Each Dawn I Die, The Street with No Name.*

117 KENNEDY, ARTHUR (1914–). Kennedy's weak mouth and slightly pained expression has made him a natural choice for unsympathetic roles not positive enough to be called "heavy": admiring young crook and Bogart's helper in *High Sierra*, boy's sceptical and

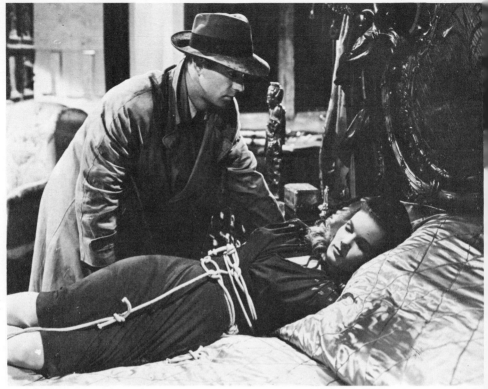

Alan Ladd and Veronica Lake in THIS GUN FOR HIRE

uninterested father in *The Window*.

Films: *High Sierra, Highway West, Boomerang, The Window, Chicago Deadline, The Desperate Hours, Crashout*.

118 KILEY, RICHARD (1922–   ). Mild-looking trader in military secrets in Sam Fuller's *Pick Up on South Street*—and most recently an excellent Don Quixote in the hit musical *Man of La Mancha*.

Films: *The Mob/Remember That Face, The Sniper, Pick Up on South Street, The Blackboard Jungle, The Phenix City Story, Pendulum*.

119 KLEINER, HARRY. Scriptwriter, occasional producer.

Films: *Fallen Angel, The Street with No Name, The Garment Jungle* (also produced), *House of Bamboo, Cry Tough* (also prod.), *Bullitt* (with Alan R. Trustman).

120 LADD, ALAN (1913–1964). Diminutive American leading man in some Forties thrillers of mixed quality. Often cast with Veronica Lake as a trench-coated gunman and the girl who changes his life. "Ladd is hard, bitter and occasionally charming, but he is after all a small boy's idea of a tough guy." (Raymond Chandler).

Films: *This Gun for Hire, Lucky Jordan, The Glass Key* (1943), *Salty O'Rourke, The Blue Dahlia, The Great*

Gatsby (1949), *Chicago Deadline, Appointment with Danger, Hell on 'Frisco Bay, 13 West Street.*

121 LAMBERT, JACK. Narrow-eyed and brutal heavy, copy-book henchman and hood.

Films: *The Killers* (1946), *Dick Tracy's Dilemma, The Enforcer/Murder Inc., 99 River Street, Kiss Me Deadly, Chicago Confidential, Hot Car Girl, Machine Gun Kelly, The George Raft Story/Spin of a Coin.*

122 LANCASTER, BURT (1913–). Nobody seeing Lancaster in his first role, as the submissive victim in Siodmak's *The Killers*, could have guessed at his future eminence, but through his many thrillers there has been

a steady progression in skill and authority.

Films: *The Killers* (1946), *I Walk Alone, Brute Force, Kiss the Blood off My Hands, Criss Cross, Mr. 880, The Young Savages, Birdman of Alcatraz.*

123 LANDERS, LEW (1901–1962). A graduate, like George Seitz, of the serials, and smooth director of *genre* films.

Films: *Parole, Condemned Women, Smashing the Rackets, Law of the Underworld, Murder in Times Square, Alias Boston Blackie, After Midnight with Boston Blackie, Crime Incorporated, Arson Squad, The Power of the Whistler, A Close Call for Boston Blackie, Chain Gang, State Penitentiary, Revenue Agent, Man in the Dark, Hot Rod Gang.*

124 LANG, FRITZ (1890–). German director who made himself master of the gangster thriller in silent days with his Dr. Mabuse films and *Spies* (1928), with Rudolf Klein-Rogge as an omnipotent criminal mastermind. In America, he created some masterly thrillers that explore in detail the seedy underside of the city.

Films: *M* (1931), *You Only Live Once, You and Me, The Big Heat, While the City Sleeps, Beyond a Reasonable Doubt.*

125 LAWRENCE, MARC (1910–). Sly, dapper U.S. actor of Thirties and Forties whose hair-line moustache and pock-marked face have become unforgettable trade-marks. He is Ziggy in *Key Largo,* the contact for whom Robinson and his gang wait, and the small-time hoodlum in *The Asphalt Jungle* who puts together the big job. For sheer malice, his performance in *Charlie Chan at the Wax Museum,* where he is a fugitive homicide indistinguishable from the Chamber of Horrors figures around him, is hard to beat.

Films: *San Quentin* (1937), *I Am the Law, Sergeant Madden, Homicide Bureau, Dust Be My Destiny, Johnny Apollo, Invisible Stripes, Charlie Chan at the Wax Museum, Public Enemies, Lady Scarface, This Gun for Hire, Eyes of the Underworld, Dillinger, I Walk Alone, Key Largo, The Asphalt Jungle, Black Hand, Vacanze Col Gangster* (in Italy), *Johnny Cool.*

At right : Marc Lawrence.
Below : Henry Fonda in
Lang's YOU ONLY LIVE ONCE

Paul Muni (convict at right) in LeRoy's
I WAS A FUGITIVE FROM A CHAIN GANG

126 LEONARD, SHELDON (1907–). American actor, now TV producer. "Harry the Horse" in *Guys and Dolls,* Leonard was the stereotype Chicago mobster, all yellow silk shirts and Runyon drawl. He underplayed nicely as the businesslike gang boss moving in on Barry Sullivan in *The Gangster,* and has made occasional guest shots in his own "Calvada Productions," including one hilarious episode of *The Dick Van Dyke Show* in which he was mobster Max Calvada trying to buy a spot for his unfunny nephew in the comedy business.
Films: *Another Thin Man, Buy Me That Town, Lucky Jordan, The Falcon in Hollywood, Crime Incorporated, Somewhere in the Night, The Gangster, Force*

of Evil, Young Man with Ideas, Stop, You're Killing Me!, Guys and Dolls, A Pocketful of Miracles.

127 LERNER, IRVING (1909–). American director, formerly director and cameraman on documentaries. His two low budget ($125,000 each) films in 1958 starring Vince Edwards were financial successes, but earned him little prominence despite their cool skill and cynical realism.
Films: *City of Fear, Murder by Contract, Man Crazy.*

128 LEROY, MERVYN (1900–). Director who, along with Michael Curtiz,

built Warner Brothers Thirties' reputation for taut, cheap thrillers. Beginning as an idealistic young director, he was instrumental in forming the Warners' reliance on natural locations, shooting *Little Caesar* in the slums and streets of American cities at a time when they were at their most unglamorous. His departure for Metro in the late Thirties meant a change to production, and to films, mainly romances and melodramas, quite untypical of his early triumphs. *The F.B.I. Story* unhappily made no attempt to return to the style of those evocative crime dramas of the early sound era.

Films: *Numbered Men, Little Caesar, Big City Blues, I Am a Fugitive from a Chain Gang, Hard To Handle, High Pressure, Two Seconds, Three on a Match, Johnny Eager, Any Number Can Play, The F.B.I. Story* (also produced).

129 LEWIS, JOSEPH H. (1900–   ). American director, creator of some classic *films maudit*. Now that the critics have discovered Fuller, one wonders how long it will take them to recognise Lewis as his

Above: Brian Donlevy, Lee Van Cleef, and Earl Holliman in Lewis's THE BIG COMBO. Opposite: Vince Edwards (rear) in Lerner's MURDER BY CONTRACT

stylistic equal and intellectual competitor. Most expert at illuminating the shady underside of the sexual impulse, Lewis peoples his films with fetishists and haunted men: George Macready desperately shredding Nina Foch's lingerie with a razor in *My Name Is Julia Ross*, gun fetishist John Dall in *Gun Crazy* lusting after side-show sharp-shooter Peggy Cummins and forging with her a perverted but enduring relationship, crusading cop Cornel Wilde in *The Big Combo* exposed to the mob through his infatuation with a night club singer.

Films: *Boys of The City, My Name Is Julia Ross, So Dark the Night, The Falcon in San Francisco, The Undercover Man, Gun Crazy, Lady without a Passport, The Big Combo.*

130 LOM, HERBERT (1917–   ). Suave Czech-born actor, popular villain in British dramas.

Films: *Dual Alibi, Night and the City, Cage of Gold, The Ladykillers, Hell Drivers, No Trees in the Street, Passport To Shame.*

131 LORRE, PETER (1904–1964). Pop-eyed European actor who was seldom well-used by Hollywood, except in horror films. His gangster pictures are variable, though in the "Mr. Moto" series, based on John P. Marquand's Asian detective and directed mostly by Norman Foster, he was occasionally funny. His gem is the effeminate Joel Cairo in Huston's *The Maltese Falcon.*

Films: *M* (1931), *Think Fast Mr. Moto, Thank You Mr. Moto, Mr. Moto's Gamble, Mr. Moto Takes a Chance, Mr. Moto on Danger Island, Mr. Moto's Last Warning, Mr. Moto Takes a Vacation,*

*At right: Herbert Lom
in THE LADYKILLERS*

*Peter Lorre as Asian detective Mr. Moto, with Virginia Field and
Thomas Beck in THINK FAST MR. MOTO*

Mr. District Attorney, The Maltese Falcon (1941), *All Through the Night, Black Angel, The Chase* (1946), *Casbah* (remake of *Algiers*), *Quicksand, Beat the Devil.*

132 LOY, MYRNA (1905–   ). A provocative *femme fatale* long before becoming the quintessential Mum of Forties films. Best as the witty Nora Charles, foil to William Powell in the "Thin Man" series.

Films: *The Girl from Chicago, Midnight Taxi, Hush Money, The Wet Parade, Manhattan Melodrama, The Thin Man, Whipsaw, After the Thin Man, Another*
Thin Man, Shadow of the Thin Man, The Thin Man Goes Home, Song of the Thin Man.

133 LUPINO, IDA (1918–   ). Small and intense British actress who, after a series of brittle roles as molls and victims in American films, became the sole female director of any skill in Hollywood. Lately active in TV.

Films: as actress: *The Lone Wolf Spy Hunt, The Lady and the Mob, They Drive by Night, Out of the Fog, High Sierra, Road House, On Dangerous Ground, Beware My Lovely, Private Hell 36* (also wrote, with Collier Young), *Women's*

Prison, While the City Sleeps. As director: *Hard Fast and Beautiful, The Hitch-Hiker.*

134 MACLANE, BARTON (1902–).

Stock U.S. henchman, solid, monotoned, often cast as a cop, especially in the "Torchy Blane" series of the late Thirties where he was Glenda Farrell's detective boyfriend. One of his better roles in a long list of unremarkable ones was as the crooked cop in the brutal *Kiss Tomorrow Goodbye,* with Cagney.

Films: *The Case of the Curious Bride, G-Men, The Case of the Lucky Legs, The Frisco Kid, Jailbreak, Bullets or Ballots, You Only Live Once, San Quentin* (1937), *You and Me, Prison Break, I Was a Convict, Big Town Czar, Mutiny in the Big House, Gangs of Chicago, The Maltese Falcon* (1941), *All through the Night, The Crime Doctor's Strangest Case, San Quentin* (1946), *Red Light, Kiss Tomorrow Goodbye, Jail Busters, The Man Is Armed, Girl on the Run.*

135 MACMAHON, HORACE (1906–).

Frog-faced U.S. actor, with voice to match. As Lt. Monaghan in *Detective Story* and the police lieutenant in the long-running TV series *Naked City* he made a niche for himself that nobody else could fill.

Films: *When G-Men Step In, Sergeant Madden, Jailhouse Blues, Waterfront at Midnight, Lady Scarface, Lady Gangster, Detective Story, Man in the Dark, Duffy of San Quentin, The Blackboard Jungle, Never Steal Anything Small, The Detective.*

136 MAFIA.

From a Sicilian word meaning well-dressed, stylish, used to describe the Sicilian-founded but now international crime movement which has dominated American organised crime since 1900s. Lately the American organisation has taken the name "La Cosa Nostra," or "Our Thing." Also known in the Twenties and Thirties as "The Black Hand."

Mafiosi first came to America at the turn of the century and started extortion rackets in New York. Richard Wilson's *Pay Or Die* tells of Joseph Petrosino who investigated them, and was murdered on a visit to Italy. *Black Hand* (Richard Thorpe, 1950) dealt with the same period.

Capone was closely associated with the Mafia, though often in conflict with them. In 1929 he called a Mafia conference in New York and suggested a national crime federation for mutual assistance. Out of this grew the illegal betting ring which was the gangs' main source of income after the repeal of Prohibition, and "Murder Inc.," the professional murder service of organised crime (see entry 150).

The Mafia in America was run through the Thirties by "Lucky" Luciano until, in 1936, he was convicted by special investigator Thomas Dewey on compulsory prostitution charges (basis of the film *Marked Woman*), jailed, then deported to Sicily in 1946, from where he continued to run the organisation. Today, the Mafia has control over many industries and essential services as well as gambling and other illegal activities.

A lack of information and the natural caution of Hollywood cinema has limited the number of films on the Mafia. *Inside the Mafia* (1959) was based on the murder of Albert Anastasia in 1957, part of an internal Mafia feud, and *Johnny Cool* (1963) combined a brutal story of revenge with details of Mafia involvement in advertising and other legitimate businesses. *Mafioso* (1962), an Italian film serio-comic in its picture of the organisation's methods of recruitment

*Still from THE SICILIAN CLAN, with
Alain Delon (running at centre rear)*

and murder, and *Salvatore Giuliano* (1962), a brilliant quasi-documentary on the famous Sicilian bandit and the political, social and economic realities of the Mafia-dominated country that produced him, took a serious look at the problem, as did *Mafia* (1949), with a script by Federico Fellini and Giuseppe Mangioni. Less concerned, two recent French films, *Je Vous Salue Mafia* (1966) with Henry Silva, and *Le Clan des Siciliens* (1969) were dramas with Mafia background, while in the U.S. *The Brotherhood* (1968) showed shifting patterns in the Cosa Nostra as old ways are replaced by new and killing gives way to accounting.

137 MANN, ANTHONY (1906–1967). Expert American director of Westerns and a number of gritty black-and-white thrillers, violent and realistic.

Films: *Strangers in the Night, Desperate* (also story, with Dorothy Atlas), *Railroaded, T-Men* (also story, uncredited, with John C. Higgins), *Raw Deal, Border Incident, Side Street*. Mann also prepared many scenes for Alfred Werker's *He Walked by Night* (1948) and wrote part of the script of Richard Fleischer's *Follow Me Quietly* (1949).

*Over page : Dennis
O'Keefe in T-MEN*

77

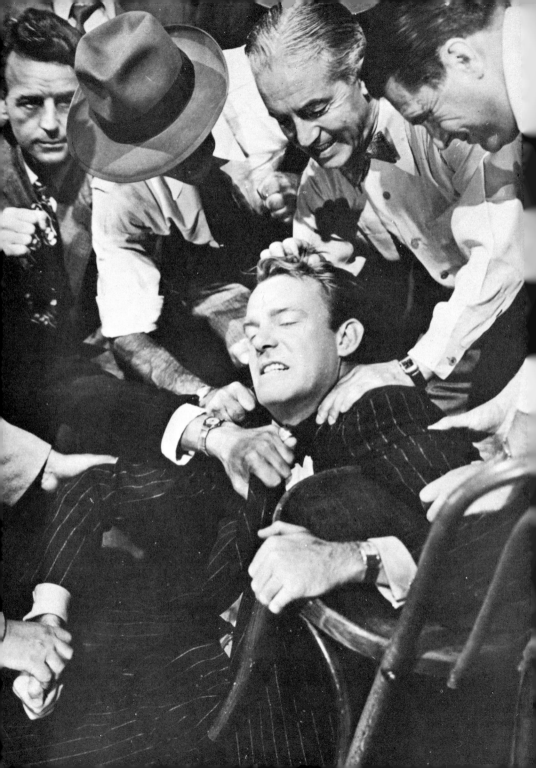

138 MARVIN, LEE (1924–   ). *The* heavy in Fifties gangster films, a snarl with a juggernaut behind it. A little gawky for his roles as the trained killer in *The Big Heat* and Chino the bikie in *The Wild One*, he expanded to encompass the complexity of the professional executioner in Siegel's *The Killers* and the overpowering ferocity of the enigmatic Walker in John Boorman's *Point Blank*. "At last, a real man." (Jeanne Moreau).

Films: *The Big Heat, The Wild One, Violent Saturday, Pete Kelly's Blues, A Life in the Balance, I Died a Thousand Times, The Killers* (1964), *Bad Day at Black Rock, Point Blank.*

Was violent detective in TV series, *M Squad.*

139 MATURE, VICTOR (1915–   ). U.S. leading man in many gangster films. Mature's almost feminine mouth makes his status as a tough guy a matter of continuing doubt. Most effective as the fearful informer in *Kiss of Death,* haunted by the spectre of the mob's grinning killer, a sadistic Richard Widmark, his campy Doctor Omar in von Sternberg's *The Shanghai Gesture* made better use of his limp charm.

Films: *Hot Spot/I Wake Up Screaming, The Brasher Doubloon/The High Window, Kiss of Death, Cry of the City, Red Hot and Blue, Gambling House, The Las Vegas Story, Dangerous Mission, Violent Saturday, The Long Haul* (in U.K.), *Interpol* (in U.K.).

140 MAYO, ARCHIE (1898–1968). Warner Brothers director of competent Thirties films, including a stagey version of Robert Sherwood's *The Petrified Forest*, with Bogart as gangster Duke Mantee.

Films: *A Doorway to Hell, Illicit, Night after Night, The Mayor of Hell,*

The Case of the Lucky Legs, The Petrified Forest (re-made 1945 as *Escape in the Desert*), *The House across the Bay, Angel on My Shoulder*.

141 MAZURKI, MIKE (1909–   ). U.S. heavy, usually dense henchman.

Films: *Murder My Sweet/Farewell My Lovely, Mysterious Intruder, Killer Dill, I Walk Alone, The Noose Hangs High, Night and the City, Dark City, Criminal Lawyer, New York Confidential, Riot on Pier 6, A Pocketful of Miracles*.

142 McGRAW, CHARLES (1914–   ). Square-jawed American actor who gives his roles as cop or gunman a stolid power. Well cast as one of the murderers in *The Killers* (1946) and as cop ferrying a witness across country in *The Narrow Margin*.

Films: *The Killers* (1946), *The Gangster, T-Men, Border Incident, The Threat, Side Street, Armored Car Robbery, His Kind of Woman, The Narrow Margin, Road Block, Loophole, Slaughter on Tenth Avenue, The Busy Body, In Cold Blood, Pendulum*.

143 MEEKER, RALPH (1920–   ). U.S. actor, the most effective of all Mike Hammers in Aldrich's *Kiss Me Deadly*.

Films: *Code Two, Big House U.S.A., Kiss Me Deadly, The St. Valentine's Day Massacre* (as Bugs Moran), *The Detective*.

144 MELVILLE, JEAN-PIERRE (1917–   ). Melville's Americophilia shows not only in his adopted name but in the style of his films, often distilling the essence of the gangster mystique.

Films: *Le Doulos/The Finger Man, L'Aîné des Ferchaux/Magnet of Doom, Le Deuxième Souffle* (also script with José Giovanni), *Le Samourai* (also script).

145 MEYER, EMILE (1903?–   ). U.S. character heavy, seldom given the opportunity to show his paces. Two sides of his *persona* were the humane warden in *Riot in Cell Block 11,* and the brutal cop who beats up Tony Curtis's Sidney Falco in *Sweet Smell of Success*.

Films: *Panic in the Streets, The Mob/Remember That Face, Riot in Cell Block 11, The Human Jungle, Shield for Murder, The Blackboard Jungle, The Man with the Golden Arm, Baby Face Nelson, The Line Up, The Case against Brooklyn, The Fiend Who Walked the West* (Western re-make of *Kiss of Death*), *Revolt in the Big House, Young Dillinger*.

146 MITCHUM, ROBERT (1917–   ). American leading man whose description of himself, "a ray of hope for

Above : Jean-Pierre Melville (right) on the set of LE SAMOURAI.
Below : Robert Montgomery in THE EARL OF CHICAGO

the great unwashed," seems atypical of his independent, thinking-man-of-action roles. A pity he never played Philip Marlowe; in build, style and voice he seems natural for Chandler's philosophical private eye.

Films: *Out of the Past/Build My Gallows High, The Big Steal, His Kind of Woman, The Racket* (1951), *Macao, Second Chance, Thunder Road* (also story), *Cape Fear.*

147 MONTGOMERY, ROBERT

(1904–). Thirties leading man who turned director in the Forties with, among other films, a subjective-camera version of *The Lady in the Lake* that develops an eerie suspense.

Films: as actor: *The Big House, The Earl of Chicago.* As director and actor:

The Lady in the Lake, Ride the Pink Horse, Eye Witness (in U.K.).

148 MORRIS, CHESTER (1902–1970). Square-jawed U.S. character actor, most famous as ex-safecracker adventurer Boston Blackie in films based on Jack Boyle's character. In 1955, he had a change of pace as humanitarian warden of Chino prison farm in *Unchained*.

Films: *The Big House, Corsair, The Miracle Man, Public Hero No. 1, Law of the Underworld, Smashing the Rackets, Meet Boston Blackie, Boston Blackie Goes Hollywood, Alias Boston Blackie, Boston Blackie's Rendezvous, Boston Blackie Booked on Suspicion, Boston Blackie and the Law, Trapped by Boston Blackie, Boston Blackie's Chinese Venture, Unchained*.

149 MUNI, PAUL (1895–   ). Versatile U.S. actor who was an impressive Capone in Howard Hawks's *Scarface*. He was to have played Bogart's role in *High*

Sierra, but argued instead for a life of Beethoven and broke with Warner Brothers as a result.

Films: *I Am a Fugitive from a Chain Gang, Scarface, Angel on My Shoulder, Stranger on the Prowl* (in Italy).

150 "MURDER INCORPORATED." Arrested in 1939 and questioned as part of a three year investigation into crime in Brooklyn conducted by District Attorney William O'Dwyer, New York criminal Abe "Kid Twist" Reles revealed that since the early Thirties he had been a paid killer for a murder ring set up by the big gangs to carry out executions, part of a service begun by Al Capone and the Mafia in 1929. Reles and his associates had worked in city groups, accepting "contracts" from interstate gangs to "hit" people they had never seen and whose offence they never knew. The result was untraceable murder without motive.

Journalist Harry Feiney first suggested the parallels of this organisation with big business, and the name "Murder Incorporated" was coined, later to be used and made famous when Burton Turkus, one of O'Dwyer's investigators, wrote a book with this title in which he told of Reles's inquisition, revelations and eventual death.

Following leads provided by Reles and others, investigators found fifty-six corpses buried in rural New York and New Jersey, but Reles set the total as higher than 130. He named Albert Anastasia and Joe Adonis as the leaders of the ring, and as their executives Louis Buchalter, known as "Louis Lepke," Louis Capone and Lepke's close associate Emanuel "Mindy" Weiss. All immediately went into hiding, and might have remained so, protected by the gangs, had public outcry not forced the F.B.I.

Stuart Whitman in MURDER INC.

to intervene, breaking its tacit agreement with the gangs not to interfere in the massive organised crime industry. Hoover made it known that he could not guarantee the gangs' continued immunity from federal pressure if a scapegoat was not disgorged, and the mob obliged with Lepke, who came out of hiding on August 24, 1939, giving himself up, by arrangement, to columnist Walter Winchell, Hoover's close friend.

As Lepke, Weiss and Capone went to trial, the gangs moved belatedly to close off the remaining sources of information. Reles died in a fall from the Coney Island hotel where he was under heavy police guard, and those who had sheltered Lepke and his friends were murdered. All three defendants were convicted, and the breach in the wall of silence surrounding organised crime discreetly closed.

First film on the conspiracy was *The Enforcer/Murder Inc.* (1951), with Bogart as the crusading D.A., Zero Mostel as the sweating informer. The film was relentless in its description of murder methods—ice-pick in the spine, shot-gun blast—and in evidence like a mass grave containing dozens of pairs of shoes. (By coincidence, Bogart had also played a part based on Dewey in *Marked Woman* (1937), suggested by the arrest of "Lucky" Luciano on compulsory prostitution charges.) A second film, *Murder Inc.,* was made in 1961, with Stuart Whitman and Mai Britt as S. K. and R. Salles, the couple who hid Lepke on gang orders. The wife was murdered, and her husband turned informer. Peter Falk was brilliantly cast as Reles. *New York Confidential* (1955) also dealt with an incident based on Lepke and his surrender.

151 NAISH, J. CARROL (1900–). American actor of slightly oriental features who is usually cast as Asian menace or gang leader.

Films: *Scotland Yard, Homicide Squad, The Beast of the City, Two Seconds, The Mouthpiece, The Mad Game, Special Agent, Tip-Off Girls, Front Page Woman, Prison Farm, Think Fast Mr. Moto, Persons in Hiding, Bulldog Drummond in Africa, Queen of the Mob, Black Hand, New York Confidential, Violent Saturday, The Young Don't Cry, The Hanged Man.*

152 NOLAN, LLOYD (1903–). Ubiquitous American actor, most often as detective, private or governmental. Was effective as private eye Mike Shayne in a series in the Forties, as an F.B.I. man hunting Nazi spies in *The House on 92nd Street,* and as a brutal gang chief in *Johnny Apollo.*

Films: *G-Men, King of Gamblers, Dangerous To Know, Undercover Doctor, Johnny Apollo, The House across the Bay, Gangs of Chicago, Michael Shayne Private Detective, Buy Me That Town, Blue White and Perfect, Dressed to Kill, Time To Kill, The House on 92nd Street, Somewhere in the Night, The Lady in the Lake, The Street with No Name, The Lemon Drop Kid* (1951), *The Girl Hunters.*

153 NOVAK, KIM (1933–). U.S. actress of Fifties, adequate romantic interest in some crime dramas, especially Richard Quine's *Pushover,* where she seduces Fred MacMurray into a robbery.

Films: *Pushover, Five against the House, The Man with the Golden Arm.*

154 O'BRIEN, EDMOND (1915–). American actor, also director. One could be forgiven for thinking that the key to O'Brien's successful career as a heavy is his ability to sweat; as the desperate poison victim in *D.O.A.,* the hostage of a madman in *The Hitch-Hiker,* the racketeer in *Pete Kelly's Blues* he exuded gallons of perspiration. A certain snarl in his voice has helped him in his gang-boss roles, one of the best being "Fats" (formerly "Slim") Murdock in *The Girl Can't Help It*, but he was equally comfortable on the other side of the law as the D.A. in *The Turning Point* caught in a web of personal involvement.

Films: *The Killers* (1946), *D.O.A.*, *White Heat*, *Backfire/Somewhere in the City*, *Between Midnight and Dawn/Prowl Car*, *711 Ocean Drive*, *The Turning Point*, *The Hitch-Hiker*, *Man in the Dark*, *Shield for Murder* (co-directed with Howard W. Koch), *Pete Kelly's Blues*, *A Cry in the Night*, *The Girl Can't Help It*, *Birdman of Alcatraz*, *The Hanged Man*.

155 O'BRIEN, PAT (1899–   ). Staccato-voiced American actor, Warner's graduate. Often cast as crusading newsman following his successful role in *The Front Page*.

Films: *Hell's House*, *The Public Enemy's Wife*, *San Quentin* (1937), *Angels with Dirty Faces*, *Dust Be My Destiny*, *Slightly Honorable*, *Castle on the Hudson*, *Crack-Up*, *Johnny One-Eye*, *A Dangerous Profession*, *Criminal Lawyer* (1951), *Inside Detroit*.

156 PALANCE, JACK (1920–   ). Skull-faced American actor who seldom conveys more than ferocity mixed with cunning. His most interesting role was a

Below : Pat O'Brien (right) with James Cagney in ANGELS WITH DIRTY FACES

Below : Jack Palance in HOUSE OF NUMBERS

double one in Russell Rouse's *House of Numbers* as convicted criminal and "straight" brother who replaces him in prison.

Films: *Panic in the Streets, Second Chance, I Died a Thousand Times, The Man Inside* (in U.K.), *House of Numbers, Once a Thief, They Came to Rob Las Vegas* (in Europe).

157 PATRICK, NIGEL (1913–   ). Clever English actor, sometime director, with a style that sets him above his contemporaries. Excellent as the mocking adjutant in *The League of Gentlemen*, and as a Scotland Yard man in *The Informers* who tracks down the killer of one of his informers in a curiously direct study of honour among those involved with crime.

Films: *Noose, Jack of Diamonds* (also scripted), *A Prize of Gold, How To Murder a Rich Uncle* (also directed), *The Man Inside, Sapphire, The League of Gentlemen, The Informers*.

Was airport cop in TV series *Zero One*.

158 PAYNE, JOHN (1912–   ). Alan Ladd's build, Bogart's snarl, Cagney's cocky stance and Kirk Douglas's dimpled chin—Payne seems to have been put together as a substitute for all of them. Never too successful, he was good as gang-boss in *The Boss* and *Slightly Scarlet*.

Films: *Larceny, The Crooked Way, Kansas City Confidential, 99 River Street, The Secret Four, The Boss, Slightly Scarlet* (1955), *Hidden Fear*.

159 PERSOFF, NEHEMIAH (1920–   ). U.S. heavy, well used in *The Untouchables* TV series as a Chicago hoodlum and in Byron Haskin's sf thriller *The Power* as a fuzzy scientist. Able to convey almost maniacal malice, he was grimly funny as the bald deaf Little Napoleon in *Some Like It Hot*.

Films: *On the Waterfront, Al Capone, Some Like It Hot, Never Steal Anything Small, The Wild Party*.

160 PEVNEY, JOSEPH (1916–   ). Boyish actor in realist dramas of Thirties and Forties (*Body and Soul, The Street with No Name, Thieves' Highway, Outside the Wall*, etc.), Pevney graduated to tight direction of similar films: well-paced monochrome dramas with a glossy surface, the best of them *Six Bridges to Cross*, story of the $2\frac{1}{2}$ million Brink's robbery in Boston, and *Female on the Beach* with Joan Crawford terrorised by cultivated murderers Jeff Chandler and Cecil Kellaway.

Films: as director: *Shakedown, Undercover Girl, Meet Danny Wilson, Six Bridges To Cross, Female on the Beach, The Midnight Story/Appointment with a Shadow*.

161 POLITO, SOL (1892–1960). One of Warner's top cameramen in the Thirties.

Films: *I Am a Fugitive from a Chain Gang, G-Men, The Petrified Forest, Angels with Dirty Faces*.

162 POWELL, DICK (1904–1963). After a score of Warner's musicals as bland leading tenor, Powell abruptly changed his image in the mid-Forties with a series of realistic thrillers in which he was directed with skill. Later he tried production and direction, with fair results. In Robert Parrish's first film, *Cry Danger* (1951) he was trying to clear himself of a robbery charge, one method being to play Russian roulette with William Conrad's head to gain information.

Films: as actor: *Murder My Sweet/Farewell My Lovely, Cornered, Johnny O'Clock, Cry Danger, You Never Can Tell*.

*William Powell and Myrna Loy, as
Nick and Nora Charles, in a Thin Man film*

163 POWELL, WILLIAM (1892–
). For Hollywood in the Thirties,
William Powell was the personification of
urban sophistication, cunning and wit.
Whether as Philo Vance, S. S. Van
Dine's gentleman sleuth, or Dashiell
Hammett's Nick Charles, the Thin Man,
he always convinced as the one man who
seemed to know what was going on.
Dapper, neat and unfailingly clever, he
succeeded best in the hands of Curtiz and
Le Roy. If one had to choose a perfect
performance, it would come down to his
frantic conman/entrepreneur in LeRoy's
High Pressure, trying to sell artificial
rubber made of sewage, or an urbane
Vance in Curtiz's brilliant *The Kennel
Murder Case*.

Films: *as Philo Vance: *The Dragnet*,
*The Canary Murder Case**, *The Greene
Murder Case**, *The Benson Murder Case**,
Street of Chance, *Shadow of the Law*,
High Pressure, *Jewel Robbery*, *Lawyer
Man*, *Private Detective 62*, *The Kennel
Murder Case**, *The Thin Man*, *Man-
hattan Melodrama*, *After the Thin Man*,
Another Thin Man, *Shadow of the Thin
Man*, *The Thin Man Goes Home*, *Hood-
lum Saint*, *Song of the Thin Man*.

164 PRISON. The uniformity of life in
prison lacking the drama on which movies
depend, films on life in confinement have
dwelt of necessity on the glamorous
aberrations—riots, breaks and escapes.
A second less popular group shows

humanitarian methods winning over hardened criminals and cynical administrators, the most obvious example of crime film's socialist/humanist bias.

Most prison films are American, and the bulk of these are set in the larger federal jails: San Quentin and Alcatraz, one on San Francisco Bay, the second, now closed, on an island in it; Sing Sing, fifty miles north of New York city; Folsom, near Sacramento, Cal.; and Leavenworth, Kansas.

The Big House (1931) is the basic prison film, showing how unenlightened treatment brutalises a young con., keeps a reformed man in jail and leads at last to a riot. *The Criminal Code* (1931) and *20,000 Years in Sing Sing* (1932) were equally grim. *San Quentin* (1937) was an

early ray of hope, with Pat O'Brien as a warden who tries rehabilitation (it was re-made in 1946). In *The Mayor of Hell* (1933) Cagney was reforming warden of a juvenile prison. But *Each Dawn I Die* and *Invisible Stripes* offered little hope for the reformed ex-con.

Ladies of the Big House (1932) led to a string of women's prison films: *Women In Prison* (1936), *Lady in the Death House* (1942) and finally *Caged* (1950), a weepie/thriller with Eleanor Powell as a prisoner who becomes pregnant in jail. It was re-made with varying success as *Women's Prison* (1954) and *House of Women* (1962). *Girls in Prison* (1956), *So Young So Bad* and other teenage reformatory films were mediocre. Rarer but more precise were two French films,

*Still from SAN QUENTIN,
a classic among prison films*

both versions of *Prison des Femmes* (1938 and 1962), the latter by Maurice Cloché, and the English melodrama *Prison without Bars* (1938).

Escapes were an early addition to the genre, getting more elaborate year by year. *Ride a Crooked Mile* (1938) showed escape from Leavenworth, *Mutiny in the Big House* (1939), *Prison Break* (1938) and *Brute Force* (1947) prison riots leading to escape. *Escape from San Quentin* showed a break by plane, and *House of Numbers* an elaborate break from San Quentin with twin replacing twin. In Becker's *Le Trou* it was a tunnel.

Execution, usually by gas or electric chair, is a popular subject. John Wexley's play *The Last Mile,* after starring Gable and Spencer Tracy on Broadway, was filmed in 1932 with Preston Foster, and again in 1959. *Two Seconds* had wife-murderer Edward G. Robinson relive his crime and what led to it in the two seconds between when the current hit the electric chair and he died. *I Want To Live* (1958) with an Oscar role for Susan Hayward and *Cell 2455 Death Row* with William Campbell as Caryl Chessman showed the brutality of capital punishment. *Black Tuesday* (1955) with its death row opening and the climax of *Angels with Dirty Faces* with Cagney dragged screaming to his death as a warning to his young admirers are still the most powerful pictures of official death.

Humanitarians have been hard put to change conditions, but *They All Come Out* (1939) preached rehabilitation, as did *Behind the High Wall* (1956) with Tom Tully as a crooked warden. *Riot in Cell Block 11,* made at the height of prison riots in 1954 and shot inside Folsom, focused public attention on the problem, while *Unchained* (1954) about the experimental open prison of Chino, Cal., and *My Six Convicts* (1952) on psychological testing and education of convicts, underlined the lesson.

Although prison has changed, films set there still turn up, often unconventional in style or attitude. Frankenheimer's *Birdman of Alcatraz* was a parable, based on fact, of a man asserting his individuality in a hostile environment. John Boorman's *Point Blank* opened and closed on the abandoned Alcatraz, but the setting was incidental to the story of formal retribution in a criminal world stripped of its intrinsic violence. Even *Riot,* Buzz Kulik's prison film, made the break seem incidental to the psycho- and socio-sexual pressures from which it sprang.

165 PRIVATE DETECTIVES. "In real life Philip Marlowe would no more be a private detective than a university don. Your private detective in real life is usually an ex-policeman with a lot of hard practical experience and the brains of a turtle or else a shabby little hack who runs around trying to find out where people have moved to." (Raymond Chandler).

Despite Chandler's strictures, film detectives have always been figures of fantasy, beginning with Sherlock Holmes who set the pattern of brilliantly intuitive thinker, dull but funny assistant and a blundering police chief always three steps behind. Holmes, played by John Barrymore, Clive Brook, Raymond Massey, Hans Albers, Eille Norwood but best by Basil Rathbone in a series 1939–44, is the most durable of all investigators.

Writers of Twenties thrillers gave the screen a horde of new and bizarre detectives, mostly physically unconventional but uniformly urbane and intelligent. Asians were popular: Peter Lorre was Mr. Moto, Boris Karloff Mr. Wong, Warner Oland, Sidney Toler and Roland

Winters were Charlie Chan. Nero Wolfe, played by Edward Arnold, was fat, a gourmet and an orchid collector; Bonita Granville as Nancy Drew was a child investigator. S. S. Van Dine's "silly ass" high society detective Philo Vance was well done by William Powell and Grant Richards, while Warren William was tougher as Perry Mason. Glenda Farrell and Jane Wyman shared Torchy Blane, girl reporter/detective, and Lloyd Nolan was more forceful as Brett Halliday's Michael Shayne.

With Hammett and Chandler, realism took over. Humphrey Bogart, Robert Montgomery and Dick Powell played Philip Marlowe, William Powell and Myrna Loy Hammett's Thin Man and his wife, Nick and Nora Charles. In the Fifties, Mickey Spillane's brutal Mike Hammer, tough and inexorable, was recreated by Biff Elliot, Robert Bray, Ralph Meeker, Darren McGavin (in the TV series) and in *The Girl Hunters* by Spillane himself. George Peppard in *P.J./New Face in Hell,* Paul Newman in Jack Smight's *Harper/The Moving Target* and Craig Stevens in the jazz-backed *Gunn* all kept the Sixties cooking.

Some of the best detective films have been frankly fantastic. In *Grand Central Murder* (1942) Van Heflin investigates the killing of a naked girl in a private railway car called Thanatos stored permanently underground, and in *You Never Can Tell* (1951) Dick Powell is a dog reincarnated as a private eye, assisted by Joyce Holden who was formerly a horse. And in the "Girl Hunt" section of *The Band Wagon* Astaire and Charisse danced a brilliant parody of the hard-boiled private eye tale.

A sub-section of the detective class is the *Adventurer.* Half-reformed crooks or soldiers of fortune, they investigate and solve crimes for motives more obscure than profit. Suave, civilised but tough, their cavalier habits lift them above the respect for law and property that hampers the private eye. One of the smoothest actors in such roles is George Sanders, who was Leslie Charteris's The Saint in a late Thirties series, then became Michael Arlen's The Falcon almost without breaking step or changing gloves. In 1942, Sanders's brother, Tom Conway, appeared with him in *The Falcon's Brother,* and the following year took over the series for another nine films. Warren William as The Lone Wolf, Chester Morris as Boston Blackie, Jack Buchanan, Ronald Colman, John Barrymore, Ron Randell and Ray Milland as Bulldog Drummond and Walter Pidgeon as Nick Carter have all provided entertainment in similar roles.

166 PROHIBITION. On January 17, 1920, the 18th Amendment to the Constitution of the U.S.A. made it illegal to drink or manufacture alcoholic liquor in the country. The Volstead Act, as it was called, put new funds in the hands of organised crime. Income from traditional sources like gambling and prostitution was meagre compared with the profits from illegal liquor, when a few gallons of alcohol flavoured with mineral oil, burnt sugar, juniper essence or colouring could sell for ten times its original cost. The less fastidious drank wine laced with formaldehyde, or "near beer" in which the alcohol, evaporated by running over hot

Opposite : Edmond O'Brien and ex-con private detective Darren McGavin in THE OUTSIDER

A raid on bootleggers in
THE WET PARADE, with Robert Young and Jimmy Durante

plates, was restored by "needling" with pure spirit.

As a prohibitive measure the Volstead Act was a failure. Drinking increased as it became socially acceptable to flout the law, and the gangs with terrorist and extortion tactics forced illegal bar owners to sell more and more of their product. Money normally passed to the government through tax and excise was added to an inflated profit and used to expand the activities of the only organisations competent to operate outside the law, the criminal gangs. Chicago gangsterism was built on prohibition, thrived while it thrived, waned when it waned. But by the time the Amendment was repealed on December 5, 1933, the gangs were firmly established, and were never to be completely rooted out.

Prohibition gave countless new words to the language. ("Bootlegging", i.e. selling illegal liquor, was revived from a Seventeenth century custom of hiding liquor for sale to the Indians in the top of a boot. "Speakeasy" became a café where, by speaking easy, i.e. quietly, to the waiter, one could get a drink. "Hijack," for pirating somebody else's goods in transit, came from the old army order "High, Jack" or "Hands Up." There were many others.

Films on Prohibition would fill a book of their own. In George Hill's *The Secret Six,* the relationship between illegal liquor and the rise of Capone was convincingly shown. In 1932 Victor Fleming directed *The Wet Parade* from Upton Sinclair's indignant novel on how liquor could lead to murder and madness, although *Song of the Eagle* (1933) cashed in on repeal by showing how an honest brewing family fought off the influence of bootlegger Charles Bickford. John Ford's *Riley the Cop,* and John Adolfi's *The Midnight Taxi* were early films to capitalise on the combination of crime and booze, but as recently as *Some Like It Hot* the same jokes were used.

Perhaps the best is Raoul Walsh's *The Roaring Twenties* (1939), with James Cagney as a returned soldier forced into the racket by post-war slump, and unable thereafter to escape until the chastening experience of the Depression. The film, with Cagney dying in the snow after having murdered gangster Bogart as his contribution to the new decade, is an apt parable of the time and the problem.

See also CHICAGO, AL CAPONE, ST. VALENTINE'S DAY MASSACRE.

167 QUINN, ANTHONY (1915–). If you look closely at some mid-Thirties gangster films from Paramount, you can see Quinn as a hood, largely indistinguishable from the rest of the mob. In the Forties it was all grand wazirs and Indian chiefs, though in 1954 he was powerful in Victor Saville's *The*

Anthony Quinn (centre) in BULLETS FOR O'HARA

Long Wait as a Spillane character clawing his way to remembrance of his past.

Films: *Parole, Dangerous To Know, King of Alcatraz, Bulldog Drummond in Africa, Tip Off Girls, Hunted Men, King of Chinatown, Emergency Squad, Parole Fixer, Larceny Inc., Bullets for O'Hara, Roger Touhy Gangster/The Last Gangster, The Long Wait, The Naked Street, The Happening.*

168 RAFT, GEORGE (1895–   ). Like Cagney, Raft began as a dancer on Broadway, member of Texas Guinan's troupe. Like Cagney, he graduated to Warner's crime films—the two even appear together, Cagney as star, Raft as uncredited extra winning a two-step competition from him and *fiancée* Loretta Young, in *Taxi* (1932). Then Raft was the coin-flipping "Little Boy" to Muni's Capone in *Scarface,* and the two careers diverged; Raft never stopped playing his early roles. Always the gambler, the half-honest detective or, more occasionally, a cop under a cloud, he never aspired to Cagney's flexibility. When, as Spats Colombo in *Some Like It Hot,* he grabs a flipped coin from a gunman and says ruefully "Where did ya learn *that* cheap trick?" one senses a realisation on his part on just how short a distance he had come.

More conscious than most actors of his *persona,* Raft has had a long association with the real underworld, lasting from his days on Broadway to the present. In both of his biopics—*Broadway* (1942) in which he plays himself, and *The George Raft Story/Spin of a Coin* (1961) where he is portrayed by Ray Danton—his interest in and admiration of the underworld is heavily underlined.

Films: *Quick Millions, Hush Money, Taxi, Scarface, Night World, Madame Racketeer, Undercover Man, Night after Night, Pick Up, Midnight Club, The Glass Key* (1935), *She Couldn't Take It, It Had To Happen, You and Me, Each Dawn I Die, I Stole a Million, Invisible Stripes, The House across the Bay, They Drive by Night, Broadway, Johnny Angel, Nocturne, Mr. Ace, Intrigue, Race Street, Johnny Allegro, Red Light, A Dangerous Profession, Lucky Nick Cain* (in Italy), *I'll Get You for This, Loan Shark, Rogue Cop, A Bullet for Joey, Some Like It Hot.*

169 RAKSIN, DAVID (1912–   ). Restrained U.S. composer whose delicate melodies ("Laura" and theme for *The Bad and the Beautiful*) often divert attention from his moody scores for films like Joseph H. Lewis's *Lady without a Passport* and *The Big Combo.*

Films: *San Quentin* (1937), *Mr. Moto's Last Warning* (collab.), *Force of Evil, Lady without a Passport, The Secret Life of Walter Mitty, Suddenly, The Big Combo, Al Capone, Pay or Die.*

170 RAY, NICHOLAS (1911–   ). Variable American director who earned critical adulation for his half-real parables of American life, some of them gangster films or social dramas with crime overtones.

Films: *They Live by Night, Knock on Any Door, On Dangerous Ground, Party Girl.*

171 ROBINSON, EDWARD G. (1893–   ). Robinson was yet another of the Broadway actors recruited by

Opposite: George Raft with Sylvia Sidney in MR. ACE

Above : Nicholas Ray

Warners to people their crime films and thrillers of the Thirties. After creating the role of Nick Scarsi in *The Racket* on stage (a role later played by Louis Wolheim in the 1928 film version), Robinson seemed unable to escape from the brutal criminal parts handed to him, and it was not until the Forties that, in films like *Scarlet Street,* he was able to break new ground. After their success he was more often cast as a cop or thinking man who begins with good intentions but is corrupted, but he was seldom absent for long from the crime world. Over the years, from *Little Caesar* to *Seven Thieves,* Robinson changed in appearance from a dapper and compact dandy to cantankerous old bullfrog, without ever losing his menace and suggestion of shrewd intelligence.

Films: *The Hole in the Wall, Night*

Ride, Outside the Law, The Widow from Chicago, Little Caesar, Smart Money, Two Seconds, I Loved a Woman, The Little Giant, The Whole Town's Talking, Bullets or Ballots, The Last Gangster, A Slight Case of Murder, The Amazing Dr Clitterhouse, I Am the Law, Blackmail* (1939), *Brother Orchid, Larceny Inc., Key Largo, Vice Squad, Black Tuesday, A Bullet for Joey, Tight Spot, Illegal, Hell on 'Frisco Bay, Seven Thieves, Robin and the Seven Hoods, The Biggest Bundle of Them All, Grand Slam.*

172   ROONEY, MICKEY (1922–   )
Half-pint Metro star of Thirties, quintessential brash teenager, who developed into a restricted actor of crime roles in later decades. Often cast as grease-monkey or mechanic who goes wrong and after the success of Siegel's *Baby Face Nelson* as an unlikely gang boss.

Films: *Manhattan Melodrama, The Devil Is a Sissy, The Strip, Quicksand, Drive a Crooked Road, The Last Mile, Baby Face Nelson, A Nice Little Bank That Should be Robbed, The Big Operator /Anatomy of the Syndicate, Platinum High School/Rich Young and Deadly.* Also directed *My True Story* (1951).

173   ROSSEN, ROBERT (1908–1966). Top Warner's scriptwriter in the Thirties, and later director; friend of Garfield whose socialist views influenced him. In *Dust Be My Destiny* he gave the actor one of his most powerful roles as a young man nearly forced into crime by social injustice and official inertia.

Films: As scriptwriter: *Marked Woman* (with Abem Finkel), *Racket Busters* (with Leonardo Bercovici), *Dust Be My Destiny, The Roaring Twenties* (with Jerry Wald, Richard Macaulay, from Mark Hellinger story), *Out of the Fog* (with Jerry Wald, Richard Macaulay). As

Edward G. Robinson (right) with
John Carradine in THE LAST GANGSTER

director/writer: *Johnny O'Clock, Body and Soul*. As producer only: *The Undercover Man*.

174 ROUSE, RUSSELL (1916–   ). U.S. director, formerly screen-writer, often in collaboration with Clarence Greene. Created the oddity *The Thief* (1952), in which no dialogue was used, and *House of Numbers,* a memorably confusing but taut prison drama with Jack Palance in a double role.

Films: As screen-writer: *D.O.A.* (with Clarence Greene), *The Great Plane Robbery*. As director: *New York Confidential, House of Numbers, A House Is Not a Home*.

175 ROZSA, MIKLOS (1907–   ). Imaginative Hungarian-born composer of music for many U.S. crime films. "Fragmentary rhythms, sharp accents, brutal brass chords, a tough and highly rhythmic theme over a basso-ostinato." (Ken Doeckel).

Films: *The Squeaker* (1937, in U.K.), *The Killers* (1946), *Brute Force, The Naked City* (with Frank Skinner), *The Bribe, Kiss the Blood off My Hands, Criss Cross, The Asphalt Jungle, Tip on a Dead Jockey/Time for Action*.

176 RUNYON, DAMON (1884– 1946). American columnist, newsman and comedy writer on whose stories of gamblers, gangsters, guys and dolls many

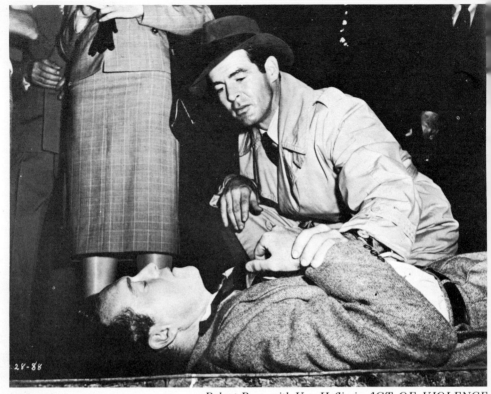

Robert Ryan with Van Heflin in ACT OF VIOLENCE

Thirties and Forties films were based. A unique dialogue style, flowery phrasing in a Brooklyn accent, and sentimental plots of gunmen reformed by lost dogs— *Johnny One Eye*—children left as security on debts—*Little Miss Marker*—and crooks co-operating to make an old beggar into a lady for her child's benefit —*Lady for a Day*—are ideal Hollywood material, as frequent re-makes testify.

Runyon-based films include: *Lady for a Day* (1933 re-made 1961 as *A Pocketful of Miracles*), *Million Dollar Ransom, The Lemon Drop Kid* (1934 re-made 1951), *A Very Honorable Guy* (1934), one of the most amusing with Joe E. Brown as an honest gambler caught by his own

ethics, *Little Miss Marker* (1934) with Shirley Temple (re-made 1949 as *Sorrowful Jones*), *A Slight Case of Murder* (1938 re-made 1953 as *Stop You're Killing Me*), *Butch Minds the Baby* (1942), *Johnny One Eye* (1949) and *Guys and Dolls* (1955). Runyon also produced some sentimental comedies and musicals in the Forties.

177 RYAN, ROBERT (1909–   ). Handsome but surly American leading man, often cast as brutal killer or man with psychological hang-up that makes him prone to violence. Excellent as the anti-Negro thief in *Odds against Tomorrow*.

Films: *Queen of the Mob, Crossfire, The Racket* (1951), *On Dangerous Ground, Beware My Lovely, Bad Day at Black Rock, House of Bamboo, Odds against Tomorrow, The Busy Body.*

178 SAINT VALENTINE'S DAY MASSACRE, THE.

Notorious Chicago gang slaying, a contributory cause of the law's crack-down on Chicago gang politics.

Early in 1929, "Bugs" Moran, who had taken over the North Side gang after Dion O'Bannion's death, began hijacking shipments of Canadian whisky brought in by a consortium of Capone's gang and the Detroit Purple Gang. Irritated, the partners set up a fake shipment and leaked the information that it would be delivered to the North Clark St. Garage at 2122 Clark St. on February 14, 1929.

A group of Moran henchmen gathered at the garage on an icy snowy morning. They were Pete Gusenberg, John May, Al Weinshank, James Clark, Adam Heyer and Dr. Reinhart H. Schwimmer, an oculist who was also Moran's fan and friend. Moran was expected momentarily, but when a car pulled up outside the garage at 10.50 a.m. it contained five men, three of them in police uniform and two who looked like plainclothesmen. Covering Moran's men with machine guns, they ordered them to face the wall

Still from Corman's THE ST. VALENTINE'S DAY MASSACRE

99

for a search. As they did so, all six were mown down with more than one hundred bullets. Two who did not die immediately were given the *coup de grâce* with a shotgun. The men left the garage at 10.58, the three uniformed men covering the other two as if an arrest had just been made. The few witnesses were duped, and nobody was able to describe the men.

The only victim to remain alive was Gusenberg, but despite wounds from fourteen bullets he refused to inform on the killers. He died a few minutes later. However it was soon common knowledge that the killers had been two imported gunmen from the St. Louis Egan's Rats mob, Fred Burke and James Ray, a Mafia man named Joseph Lolordo, and two Chicago hoods, John Scalise and Albert Anselmi. The ingenious plan had been worked out by "Machine Gun" Jack McGurn, Capone's most efficient and trusted killer.

McGurn was arrested and tried, but released for lack of evidence. In May 1929, at Spooners Nook, Indiana, a car was found containing the bodies of Scalise, Anselmi and Joseph Giunta, all presumably shot by Moran's men. Aside from this rough justice, the St. Valentine's Day killers were never punished.

Recorded with varying degrees of accuracy, the incident has been shown in a number of films: Richard Wilson's *Al Capone*, Hawks's *Scarface*, Roger Corman's *The St. Valentine's Day Massacre*, and also in Billy Wilder's *Some Like It Hot,* where a dapper George Raft as "Spats" Colombo rubs out "Toothpick Charlie" (George E. Stone).

179   SAWYER, JOSEPH (1908–   ). Stock Warner's henchman, the ex-Army sergeant on whom Bogart revenges himself during a hold-up in *The Roaring Twenties.*

Films: *Wharf Angel, Looking for Trouble, Car 99, Special Agent, The Petrified Forest, San Quentin* (1937), *The Lady and the Mob, The Roaring Twenties, You Can't Get Away with Murder, The Lucky Stiff, The Killing.*

180   SEARS, FRED F. (1913–1957). American director of Z-films who did a few competent science fiction and crime films, often in association with producer Sam Katzman's Clover Productions.

Films: *The Miami Story, Chicago Syndicate, Cell 2455 Death Row, Inside Detroit, Rumble on the Docks, Escape from San Quentin, Teenage Crime Wave, Miami Exposé.*

181   SEILER, LEWIS (1891–1964). Efficient Warner's director of the Thirties, whose best later work includes a competent re-make of *Caged* (*Women's Prison*).

Films: *Crime School, King of the Underworld, You Can't Get Away with Murder, Hell's Kitchen* (with E. A. Dupont), *Dust Be My Destiny, It All Came True, The Big Shot, The System* (1953), *Women's Prison, The True Story of Lynne Stuart.*

182   SEITZ, JOHN F. (1899–   ). Top American cameraman of Forties and Fifties. Shot many Alan Ladd features.

Films: *Sergeant Madden, This Gun for Hire, Lucky Jordan, The Big Clock, The Great Gatsby* (1949), *Chicago Deadline, Appointment with Danger, Rogue Cop, Hell on 'Frisco Bay, A Cry in the Night.*

183   SIDNEY, SYLVIA (1910–   ). Thirties heroine of U.S. city films, specialising in bruised girlfriends, wan and dispirited ladies of the slums. Fragile and birdy face lent conviction to such roles as Joel McCrea's girl in

Sylvia Sidney (right) with Lee Marvin in VIOLENT SATURDAY

Mamoulian's *City Streets* and Wyler's *Dead End,* Henry Fonda's wife and Spencer Tracy's *fiancée* in Lang's *You Only Live Once* and *Fury* respectively. A Bette Davis without fire, her career died with the end of the slum drama.

Films: *City Streets, Ladies of the Big House, The Miracle Man, Pick-Up, Mary Burns Fugitive, You Only Live Once, Dead End, You and Me, Mr. Ace, Violent Saturday, Behind the High Wall.*

84 SIEGEL, DONALD (1912–   ). American director, dean of the modern cinema of violence and action. His background as a montage expert has given him an intimate knowledge of film mechanics, and of the means whereby much may be made of little. His car chase at the end of *The Line Up* and his drawing of the Eli Wallach killer Dancer broke new ground that is still being farmed by lesser men. Active in TV in the early Sixties his remake of *The Killers,* with Lee Marvin, was considered too violent for the programme that commissioned it, and finally saw release as a feature.

Films: *The Big Steal, Riot in Cell Block 11, Private Hell 36, Crime in the Streets, Baby Face Nelson, The Line Up, Edge of Eternity, The Hanged Man, The Killers* (also produced), *Madigan, Coogan's Bluff.*

*Don Siegel at rear (wearing hat) with stars
Clint Eastwood and Susan Clark on COOGAN'S BLUFF*

185 SINATRA, FRANK (1915–).
Sinatra's interest in crime films seems,
like that of Raft, to be based as much on
his admiration of and involvement in the
underworld as artistic or monetary con-
siderations. In *Guys and Dolls* he played
a character based on Arnold Rothstein,
creator of the modern organised mob
concept, and in *Suddenly* was a killer
hired to assassinate the President of the
U.S.A. More recently, in *The Detective*
and two Tony Rome films he explored
some of the complexities of modern
attitudes to crime.

Films: *Meet Danny Wilson, Suddenly,
The Man with the Golden Arm, Guys and
Dolls, The Joker Is Wild, Robin and the
Seven Hoods, Assault on a Queen, Ocean's
Eleven, Tony Rome, Lady in Cement, The
Detective.*

186 SIODMAK, ROBERT (1900–
). Austrian-born director who
created some of the most chilling Hollywood crime dramas of the Forties.
"Equivocal, obsessed with pathology,
illness and depravity, he seemed at once
to be the cinema's morbid psychologist

Portraits: Frank Sinatra (above);
Robert Siodmak (right);
and Lionel Stander (below)

and a slick extortionist of thrills."
(Charles Higham).

Films: *The Suspect, The Killers* (1946),
*The Dark Mirror, Cry of the City, Criss
Cross, The File on Thelma Jordan, De-
ported, The Rough and the Smooth (in
U.K.).*

187 STANDER, LIONEL (1908–
). Stormy petrel of U.S. heavies,
intimate of New York's Thirties intellectual elite and occasional actor in films
by Ulmer, Hecht and other controversial
talents. Excellent as the brutal hood in
The Last Gangster, and as the bemused
fleeing gunman in Polanski's *Cul-de-Sac.*

Films: *Meet Nero Wolfe, The League
of Frightened Men, The Last Gangster,
Call Northside 777, St. Benny the Dip,
The Moving Finger, Cul-de-Sac.*

Rod Steiger in ON FRIDAY AT 1!

188 STANWYCK, BARBARA (1907–). American leading lady who has hovered around the fringes of gangster film but seldom stepped in, although her portrayals in *Cry Wolf, Sorry Wrong Number* and as the corrupt and erotic murderess in *Double Indemnity* have added much to the grammar of the form. Of her few parts in gangster films, that as the torch singer "Sugarpuss" O'Shea in *Ball of Fire* is a *tour-de-force*.

Films: *The Locked Door, Illicit, Ball of Fire, The File on Thelma Jordan.*

189 STEIGER, ROD (1925–). Stocky American actor, like Muni in his adaptability to new roles and characters. Effective as Capone in Richard Wilson's biopic.

Films: *On the Waterfront, Cry Terror, Al Capone, On Friday at 11, Seven Thieves, 13 West Street.*

190 STEINER, MAX (1888–). Ubiquitous composer, staff member at Warners and RKO, who conveyed as well as anybody the rhythm of the urban world. Used pop tunes to effect in most films.

Films: *The Crime Doctor, Crime School, Angels with Dirty Faces, They Made Me a Criminal, The Big Sleep,*

White Heat, Caged, Illegal, Hell on Frisco Bay, The F.B.I. Story, Portrait of a Mobster.

191 STERLING, JAN (1923–   ). Blonde U.S. leading lady with bitter mouth. Excellently cast as one of the women prisoners in Cromwell's *Caged.*

Films: *Mystery Street, Caged, Appointment with Danger, Split Second, The Human Jungle, Women's Prison, Female on the Beach, Slaughter on Tenth Avenue, High School Confidential.*

192 STEVENS, MARK (1916–   ). U.S. actor who became director of lively crime films after roles as cop or private detective. He's the private eye framed by William Bendix in *The Dark Corner.*

Films: as actor: *Within These Walls, The Dark Corner, The Street with No Name, Between Midnight and Dawn/ Prowl Car, Cry Vengeance* (also produced and directed), *Time Table* (also produced and directed).

193 STEVENS, ROBERT (1925–   ). Talented U.S. director, ex-TV. *The Big Caper* is a clever robbery film, Rory Calhoun a mobster who lives in a town for a year to prepare for the job, James Gregory the idea man, lured away from his pool by the thought of a big caper, and James Harris as a sweating pyromaniac henchman, grimly believable. Also *Never Love a Stranger.*

Robert Stevens talks to actors Rory Calhoun and Mary Costa on THE BIG CAPER

194 STEWART, JAMES (1908–). Initially a juvenile stooge and romantic lead with M-G-M. (in *Ziegfeld Girl* he was a truck-driver turned bootlegger, in *After the Thin Man* the rotten son of a noble house, and the murderer). Stewart accepted middle age gracefully, and with it roles as a tough cop or sophisticated city boy in Hitchcock's more distinguished thrillers. Despite the tangled psychological web and visual bravura of *Vertigo,* his best film is *Call Northside 777* where he relentlessly tracks down a killer in the seedier parts of New York. *The F.B.I. Story* let him associate with every Federal case from Dillinger to the Rosenbergs, always in 'phone contact with J. Edgar Hoover.

Films: *The Murder Man, After the Thin Man, Call Northside 777, The Last Gangster, The F.B.I. Story.*

195 STEWART, PAUL (1908–). White-haired skull-faced American actor, often cast as gang-leader.

Films: *Johnny Eager, Mr. Lucky, The Window, Appointment with Danger, Loan Shark, Chicago Syndicate, Kiss M Deadly, Hell on 'Frisco Bay, The Wild Party, In Cold Blood.* Also directed *Siege* (1956).

196 STONE, LEWIS (1879–1953) U.S. actor noted for civilised portraits in Metro films of the Thirties. Judge Hardy in Hardy Family films. Most effective as drunken attorney in *The Secret Six,* sinister spy chief in *Mata Hari* with Garbo, and weary police chief in Del Ruth's *Bureau of Missing Persons.*

Films: *The Big House, The Secret Six, The Wet Parade, Bureau of Missing Persons, Don't Turn 'Em Loose, Hoodlum Saint.*

197 SULLIVAN, BARRY (1912–). U.S. leading man. One of his finest crime films is *The Gangster,* where he plays a failing mobster whose Goya-decorated apartment and obsession with cabaret singer Belita betray inner confusion and despair. Few of his other films have lived up to this.

Films: *Framed, The Gangster, The Great Gatsby* (1949), *Loophole, The Miami Story, The Purple Gang, No Questions Asked, The Way to the Gold, It Takes All Kinds* (in Australia).

198 TALBOT, LYLE (1904–   ). Soft-spoken American character actor, sometimes cast against type as gangster, to good effect. It is he who lures Ann Dvorak into the rackets in *Three on a Match* with a nice line in shipboard seduction.

Films: *A Lost Lady, Fog over 'Frisco, Three on a Match, 20,000 Years in Sing Sing, The Dragon Murder Case, The Case of the Lucky Legs, Parole Fixer, A Night for Crime, One Body Too Many, The Falcon Out West, Revenue Agent, Federal Man, Calling Homicide, High School Confidential, City of Fear.*

199 TALMAN, WILLIAM (1917–1968). Snarling U.S. heavy, prosecutor Hamilton Burger in the Perry Mason TV series, and the one-eyed kidnap killer in da Lupino's *The Hitch-hiker.*

Films: *Armored Car Robbery, The Racket* (1951), *The Hitch Hiker, The City That Never Sleeps, Big House U.S.A., The Man Is Armed.*

200 TAMIROFF, AKIM (1899–   ). Russian-born character actor, active in American and lately European thrillers. Most notable as the terrified Grandi in Welles's *Touch of Evil,* but earlier a greasy, vain and petulant gang-leader in Paramount crime films, many by Robert Florey.

Films: *King of Gamblers, Dangerous To Know, King of Alcatraz, Ride a Crooked Mile, King of Chinatown, The Gangster, Touch of Evil, Ocean's Eleven, Topkapi.*

Akim Tamiroff as Grandi in TOUCH OF EVIL

201 TAYLOR, ROBERT (1911–1969). Even as top cop Matt Holbrook in his TV series *The Detectives* (one episode, *Recoil,* seen in British cinemas), Taylor never convinced as a tough guy; that brow, however furrowed, and mouth, however pursed, never lost the image of Camille's Armand. However, as crooked lawyer in Nicholas Ray's *Party Girl* and half-bad smuggler in *Tip on a Dead Jockey/Time for Action,* he was briefly convincing.

Films: *Buried Loot* (two-reels, 1935), *Johnny Eager, High Wall, The Bribe, Rogue Cop, Tip on a Dead Jockey/Time for Action, Party Girl, House of the Seven Hawks, A House Is Not a Home.*

202 TEAL, RAY (1902–   ). U.S. heavy, expert leader of lynching mobs,

*Robert Taylor
in HIGH WALL*

but occasionally cop or jail guard.

Films: *Circumstantial Evidence, Deadline for Murder, Brute Force, The Captive City, The Turning Point, The Wild One, The Desperate Hours.*

203 TETZLAFF, THEODORE T. ("Ted") (1903–). Accomplished U.S. cameraman who later became director of effective thrillers.

Films: as cameraman: *Stool Pigeon, Attorney for the Defence, Murder with Pictures, Arrest Bulldog Drummond.* As director: *Johnny Allegro, The Window, A Dangerous Profession, Gambling House, Under the Gun.*

204 T-MEN. Tax-men, i.e. representatives of the U.S. Department of Internal Revenue who co-operated with the F.B.I. in tracking down and convicting gangsters who falsified tax records. Their work was commemorated in *T-Men* (1948), and in *White Heat* (1949), where they were James Cagney's downfall. Also *Revenue Agent* (1950), and *The Undercover Man* (1949), about the Capone tax case.

205 TOTTER, AUDREY (1919–). Poker-faced blonde of Forties films, well used by Robert Montgomery in his subjective-camera version of *The Lady in the Lake*.

Films: *Main Street After Dark, The Lady in the Lake, High Wall, Any Number Can Play, Alias Nick Beal, Under the Gun, The Sell Out, F.B.I. Girl, Man in the Dark, Women's Prison, A Bullet for Joey.*

206 TOUHY, ROGER "The Terrible" (? –1959). Ambiguous and contradictory figure of Chicago mobsterdom whose life and intrigues will probably never be unravelled. Son of a Chicago cop, Touhy entered bootlegging while still young and set up in opposition to Capone in the large Chicago suburb of Des Plaines, where his gang had absolute control. From 1926 until Capone's downfall he was a constant threat and irritation to the big gang, but all overt attempts to crush him failed, partly due to Touhy's ingenious bootlegging operations, carried out with flair and imagination—beer, for instance, was shipped in converted oil trucks painted with the colours of a well-known petrol firm.

The mystery of Touhy deepened in 1931, when Anton Cermak was elected mayor of Chicago. Touhy later claimed that he and Cermak had come to an agreement, under which Touhy and his gang would wage war on the Capone mob, with the facilities of the police department placed at his disposal. Other authorities suggest that Capone, hearing of this, had Cermak murdered soon after as he stood beside Franklin Roosevelt at a Miami election meeting, although a deranged self-confessed anarchist, Giuseppe Zingara, was arrested for the crime. The incident was the basis of an interesting two-part episode of the TV programme *The Untouchables,* and was released in some places as a feature, *The Guns of Zingara.*

In 1933, Touhy was arrested on the charge of having kidnapped con-man Jake "The Barber" Factor and, despite claims that Capone had framed him, was given a ninety-nine year sentence, obviously as part of the Federal drive to discourage kidnapping, then a popular source of bandit revenue. The evidence was slim, many of the witnesses either gangsters or fools. In 1954, the sentence was finally quashed amid charges by the examining judge of perjury, withholding evidence and bias in those who had prepared the first case. Due to a technicality, Touhy was not released until 1959, and twenty-three days after, he was shot down, one of the last victims of Capone's vengeance.

The only film on Touhy is *Roger Touhy, Gangster* (*The Last Gangster* in U.K.), an entertaining outdoor version of his life with Preston Foster which lacks most of the character's depth and avoids the more intriguing facts of his case.

207 TOURNEUR, JACQUES (1904–   ). American director, born Paris, son of Maurice Tourneur. After cutting his teeth at Metro on *Passing Parade* and *Crime Does Not Pay* shorts, Tourneur

Tourneur's NICK CARTER MASTER DETECTIVE, starring Walter Pidgeon

directed one of the latter so effectively that M-G-M allowed its extension to feature length. The result, *They All Come Out,* is an economical prison drama extolling the doubtful opportunities for rehabilitation in U.S. jails. The same year (1939) he directed two Nick Carter films, *Nick Carter Master Detective* and *Phantom Raiders,* with Walter Pidgeon as the virile sleuth and Donald Meek as his beekeeping assistant Bartholomew, the latter film notable for Joseph Schildkraut, distinguished German actor (free the week of shooting), playing an animal-loving gang-leader. More impressive is *Out of the Past/Build My Gallows High*. Few films more accurately mirror the icy tensions of the underworld as this low key drama of a leonine private eye (Robert Mitchum) in conflict with big gambler Kirk Douglas over Jane Greer, their shared mistress and nemesis. Also *Nightfall*.

208 TRACY, SPENCER (1900–1967). Father figure of American cinema who began, like many, as a journeyman character actor at Warners and Metro, grinding out his share of crime films.

These evaporated after *Captains Courageous*, Tracy's first Oscar, but in John Sturges's *Bad Day at Black Rock* he recalled some of the indomitability of those early roles.

Films: *Taxi Talks* (two-reels, 1930), *Up the River, Quick Millions, 20,000 Years in Sing Sing, Disorderly Conduct, The Mad Game, Whipsaw, They Gave Him a Gun, The Big City, Bad Day at Black Rock*.

209 TREVOR, CLAIRE (1909–   ). One of the few Thirties blondes who emerged from the period with negotiable acting credits; as the lady gang-leader in

Spencer Tracy (seated at left) menaced by Lee Marvin in BAD DAY AT BLACK ROCK. Opposite page: Claire Trevor watches Bogart and Bacall in KEY LARGO

692-90

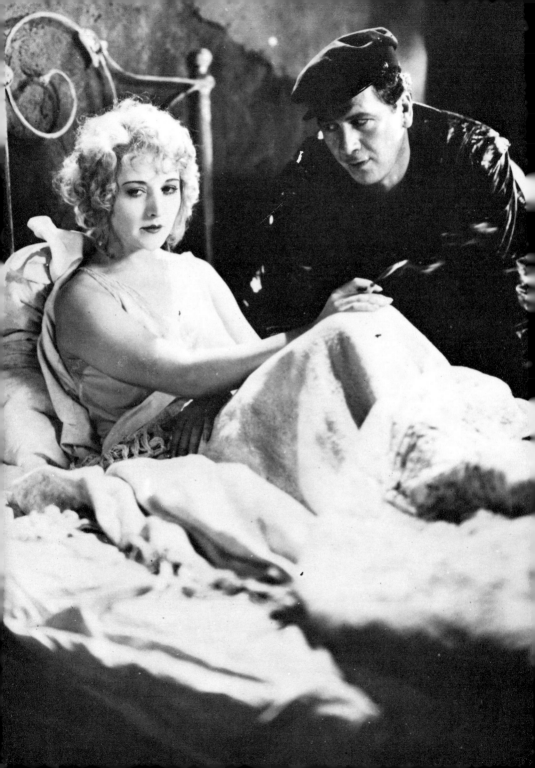

The Amazing Dr. Clitterhouse and the object of Akim Tamiroff's affections in *King of Gamblers* she was crisply believable. Later, she won a deserved Oscar for her part as the drunken floozie in *Key Largo*, and was grimly threatening in Robert Wise's *Born to Kill*.

Films: *The Mad Game, Human Cargo, King of Gamblers, Big Town Girl, Dead End, The Amazing Dr. Clitterhouse, I Stole a Million, Murder My Sweet, Johnny Angel, Crack-Up, Key Largo, The Lucky Stiff, Borderline, Hard Fast and Beautiful, Hoodlum Empire, Stop You're Killing Me!*

210 VAN DYKE, WILLIAM S. (1887–1943).

Skilled Metro director of series films, and of The Thin Man pictures with William Powell and Myrna Loy unravelling impenetrable mysteries against a background of brittle chatter and sophisticated high-life.

Films: *Night Court, Manhattan Melodrama, The Thin Man, Hide Out, The Devil Is a Sissy* (with Rowland Brown), *After the Thin Man, They Gave Him a Gun, Another Thin Man, Shadow of the Thin Man.*

211 VENTURA, LINO (1919–   ).

Solid and blocky French actor, long in French crime films. Extremely convincing in *Classe Tous Risques/The Big Risk* as ageing hold-up man on the run with two children.

Films: *Touchez Pas au Grisbi, Razzia Sur la Chnouf, La Loi des Rues, Maigret Tend un Piège/Maigret Sets a Trap, Cent Mille Dollars au Soleil/Greed in the Sun, Classe Tous Risques/The Big Risk, Cloportes, Le Deuxième Souffle, L'Arme à Gauche/Guns for the Dictator, Le Clan des Siciliens.*

212 VON STERNBERG, JOSEF (1894–1970).

Quirky and brilliant American director, creator of some of cinema's most exquisite visual delights. His *Underworld* and *The Docks of New York* show a poet's response to the grime of the urban underside, a Baudelaire-ian view of corruption and despair.

Films: *Underworld, The Dragnet, The Docks of New York, Thunderbolt, Sergeant Madden, Macao.*

213 WALSH, RAOUL (1889–   ).

Powerful U.S. director, master of urban melodrama, spectacle and mordant comedy, *genres* which at Warner Brothers in the Thirties and Forties he had ample opportunity to direct. Few people squeezed more from Bogart and Cagney, who in *The Roaring Twenties* came together under his direction to create one of the basic gangster films.

Films: *Me Gangster, The Bowery, Baby Face Harrington, The Roaring Twenties, They Drive by Night, High Sierra, Salty O'Rourke, White Heat* (re-made 1958 as *The Law vs. Gangster*), *The Enforcer/Murder Inc.* (credited to Bretaigne Windust but actually Walsh).

214 WANGER, WALTER (1894–1968).

Independent American producer. His own experience in prison where he served a sentence in the late Forties on a charge of wounding a man over his wife Joan Bennett led to two of the most critical anti-prison films, *Riot in Cell Block 11* and *I Want To Live*.

Films: *Mary Burns Fugitive, You Only Live Once, Algiers, Riot in Cell Block 11, I Want To Live.*

Opposite: Betty Compson and George Bancroft in von Sternberg's THE DOCKS OF NEW YORK

215 WARNER, JACK (1900–). English actor whose roles as London bobby and inspector (*The Blue Lamp, Jigsaw, The Ladykillers*) overshadow his brilliant playing as a brutal escaped convict in Alfred Roome's *My Brother's Keeper*.

216 WEBB, ROY. Composer of scores for many RKO films, including all Val Lewton's horror classics, others by Hitchcock (*Notorious*) and Siodmak (*The Spiral Staircase*). Deceptively simple, his musical backgrounds are in marked contrast to the florid arrangements typical of the crime film.

Films: *Full Confession, The Saint Strikes Back, Seven Miles from Alcatraz, Mr. Lucky, The Falcon in Danger, The Falcon Strikes Back, The Falcon's Brother, Dick Tracy, Crossfire, Out of the Past/Build My Gallows High, The Window, Dangerous Mission, Gambling House*.

217 WELLMAN, WILLIAM A. (1896–). At Warners in the early Thirties, Wellman was the most powerful and deeply committed of the studio's socially conscious directors. In *The Public Enemy*, which made Cagney's reputation, he seemed unable to create a workable synthesis of the gangster myth and his own disgust at crime and its effect on society; as a result, the film is often laboured and obvious, despite its superbly horrific final climaxes, the gunfight in the rain and Cagney's delivery to his family's doorstep, a swaddled corpse. More to be praised is *The Steel Highway,* again with Cagney, a drama of life on the railroads with some brilliant Barney McGill camerawork, and *Wild Boys of the Road*, a Marxist parable to rank with the great revolutionary works. Adapted from Soviet director Nikolai Ekk's *The Road to Life*, it shows the Depression to be America's proletarian revolution, and the roving gangs of orphan children as the forerunners of a mob who would, handled with less understanding, have swept away the American government.

Films: *Ladies of the Mob, The Public Enemy, The Star Witness, Wild Boys of the Road*. Also part script on *The Last Gangster*.

218 WIDMARK, RICHARD (1915–). American actor. Statistically his roles as cop or private citizen outnumber those in which he has played a sadistic killer, but, perhaps regrettably, Widmark will always be most remembered as the vicious murderer in *Kiss of Death* who says, with a chilling giggle, "*Dames* are no good if you wanna have some fun." More work seems to have gone into other roles, such as the straight lawyer in *The Trap/The Baited Trap*, weary and slightly soiled cop in *Madigan* and health officer investigating an outbreak of plague in *Panic in the Streets*.

Films: *Kiss of Death, The Street with No Name, Road House, Night and the City* (in U.K.), *Panic in the Streets, No Way Out, Pick-up on South Street, A Prize of Gold* (in Europe), *The Trap/The Baited Trap, Madigan*.

219 WILLIAM, WARREN (1893–1948). Suave leading man who was Warner Brothers' "answer" to John Barrymore in the Thirties. His roles with few exceptions were smooth adventurers, and his two most popular—as Perry Mason in the late Thirties at Warners (films marked*), and the Lone Wolf in six films based on a Michael Arlen-invented gentleman adventurer—might have been written for him. Also Philo Vance†.

Films: *The Mouth Piece, Three on a Match, The Dragon Murder Case†, The Case of the Howling Dog*, The Case of the*

*Above : Richard Widmark and Harry Guardino
threatened in Siegel's MADIGAN.
At right : Warren William*

Curious Bride, The Case of the Lucky
Legs*, The Gracie Allen Murder Case†,
Arsène Lupin Returns, The Lone Wolf Spy
Hunt, The Lone Wolf Strikes, The Lone
Wolf Meets a Lady, The Lone Wolf Keeps
a Date, The Lone Wolf Takes a Chance,
The Secret of the Lone Wolf, Eyes of the
Underworld.*

220 WILLIAMS, ADAM (—   ).
U.S. henchman, solid, smiling, dangerous.

Films: *Vice Squad, The Big Heat, The
Girl in Room 17, Crash-out, The Garment
Jungle.*

221 WINTERS, SHELLEY (1922–). Brainless cashier in *The Gangster*, pathetic floozie in *Cry of the City*, junkie in *Let No Man Write My Epitaph*, and alcoholic in *Harper/The Moving Target*, Miss Winters's talent for whining fecklessness has had liberal exercise in crime films.

Films: *The Racket Man, The Gangster, Larceny, Cry of the City, The Great Gatsby* (1949), *Johnny Stool Pigeon, He Ran All the Way, Meet Danny Wilson, I Died a Thousand Times, Odds against Tomorrow, Let No Man Write My Epitaph, A House Is Not a Home, Harper/ The Moving Target, Bloody Mama.*

222 WISE, ROBERT (1914–). Brilliant U.S. director, precise in his early films and showing an instinctive good taste in his later block-busters. His thrillers and gangster films are hypnotic exercises in action, showing his early training as an editor.

Films: *Criminal Court, Mystery in Mexico, The Captive City, I Want To Live, Odds against Tomorrow* (also produced), *West Side Story* (with Jerome Robbins).

223 WOOLRICH, CORNELL (1903–1968). American novelist who, under his own name and those of "William Irish" and "George Hopley" wrote some brilliant crime romances, all informed with a complexity of motivation and plot that has fascinated film-makers. One of the finest was *Phantom Lady*, basis of Siodmak's classic film. Others have been the raw material of Truffaut's *The Bride Wore Black* and Hitchcock's *Rear Window*.

Films: original story: *Convicted, Black Angel, The Chase* (1946), *Fall Guy, The Window.*

Shelley Winters in A DOUBLE LIFE

Peter Yates (right) with
Robert Vaughn on the set of BULLITT

224 YATES, PETER (1929–   ). English director who in his short career has produced two of the best gangster films of the last ten years. His picture of the Great Train Robbery in *Robbery* was tense and precise, with brilliant direction of Stanley Baker as the mastermind, while *Bullitt,* his first American film, gave similar scope to Steve McQueen as a Los Angeles detective pursuing the threads of a bloody power struggle among the gangs.

225 YORDAN, PHILIP. American screenwriter, lately producer.

Films: *Dillinger, The Chase* (1946, from Cornell Woolrich story *The Black Path of Fear*), *Detective Story* (with Robert Wyler from Sidney Kingsley's play), *Man Crazy* (with Sidney Harmon, also co-produced), *The Big Combo, Joe Macbeth, The Fiend Who Walked the West* (co-scripted with Harry Brown and based on a script by Ben Hecht for *Kiss of Death,* also co-produced).

Index

FILMS are listed in alphabetical order. Where a film was produced in a language other than English, it is listed under its original title, in italics. If a film has an alternative title, this appears directly after the release title. It is also listed in alphabetical order with a cross-reference to the original title.

After each title, the film's release date is given. If the director has no special entry in the book, his name is given before the date. The figures that follow refer to the numbered entries in the body of the book. They are arranged as follows: Director; actors and actresses; technicians, including cameramen, composers, editors and designers (N.B. these figures are always in italics); lastly script-writers, writers of original stories and producers or other executives.

Where the listing also includes a figure preceded by the letter "E", e.g. "E164", this indicates that a reference to the film appears in one of the general entries about personalities or classes of film. For instance, the note "E164" after the film *The Criminal Code* means that a comment on it appears in entry 164, that on Prison Films.

A

*John Garfield, William Conrad and
Joseph Pevney, in Rossen's BODY AND SOUL*

120

1951) 120, 191, 195; *182*.

Armé à Gauche/Guns for the Dictator (Claude Sautet 1967) 211.

Armored Car Robbery (1950) 77; 142, 199.

Arrest Bulldog Drummond (James Hogan 1938) *203*.

Arsène Lupin Returns (George Fitz-maurice 1938) 219.

Arson Squad (1945) 123.

Asphalt Jungle (1950) 110; 66, 100, 125; *175*; 36.

Assault on a Queen (Jack Donohue 1966) 49, 185.

Attorney for the Defence (Irving Cummings 1932) *203*.

B

Baby Face Harrington (1935) 213.

Baby Face Nelson (1957) 184; 50, 63, 113, 145, 172; E68.

Backfire/Somewhere in the City (Vincent Sherman 1950) 20, 154.

Bad Company (Tay Garnett 1932) 52.

Bad Day at Black Rock (John Sturges 1954) 29, 138, 177, 208.

Bad One (George Fitzmaurice 1930) 114; 75.

Baited Trap *see* Trap.

Ball of Fire (1941) 99; 5, 72, 188.

Beast of the City (Charles Brabin 1932) 97, 111, 151; 36.

Beat the Devil (1954) 110; 28, 131.

Behind Prison Gates (Charles Barton 1939) 70.

Behind the High Wall (Abner Biberman 1956) 183; E164.

Behind the Mask (John Francis Dillon 1932) 114.

Benson Murder Case (Frank Tuttle 1930) 163.

Bermuda Mystery (Benjamin Stoloff 1944) 83.

Between Midnight and Dawn/Prowl Car (1950) 71, 154, 192.

Beware My Lovely (Harry Horner 1952) 133, 177.

Beyond a Reasonable Doubt (1956) 124; 5.

Bidone/Swindlers (Federico Fellini 1955) 53.

Big Caper (1957) 193.

Big City (Frank Borzage 1937) 208.

Big City Blues (1932) 128; 27.

Big Clock (1948) 75; *182*.

Big Combo (1954) 129; 1, 49, 63, 70; *169*; 225.

Biggest Bundle of Them All (Ken Annakin 1966) 171.

Big Heat (1953) 124; 81, 93, 113, 138, 220.

Big House (1930) 104; 19, 147, 148, 196; E164.

Big House U.S.A. (Howard W. Koch 1955) 32, 53, 143, 199.

Big Operator/Anatomy of the Syndicate (Charles Haas 1959) 47, 58, 172.

Big Punch (1921) 82.

Big Risk *see Classe Tous Risques*.

Big Shakedown (John Francis Dillon 1933) 52, 60, 74, 112.

Big Shot (1942) 181; 28.

Big Sleep (1946) 99; 10, 28, 50; *190*; 43.

Big Snatch *see Melodie en Sous Sol*.

Big Steal (1949) 184; 23, 146.

Big Tipoff (Frank MacDonald 1955) 49.

Big Town Czar (Arthur Lubin 1939) 134.

Big Town Girl (Alfred Werker 1937) 209.

Birdman of Alcatraz (John Franken-heimer 1962) 30, 122, 154; *95*; E54,

The East Side Kids in BOYS OF THE CITY

E164.

Bishop Murder Case (1930) 94.

Black Angel (Roy William Neill 1946) 72, 131; 223.

Blackboard Jungle (1955) 34; 81, 118, 135, 145.

Black Hand (Richard Thorpe 1950) 125, 151; E136.

Blackmail (H. C. Potter 1939) 171.

Black Market Babies (1945) 17.

Black Tuesday (Hugo Fregonese 1954) 171; E164.

Blind Date/Chance Meeting (Joseph Losey 1959) 12.

Blonde Crazy (1931) 65; 38.

Blonde Ransom (1945) 17.

Blood Money (1933) 35; 13.

Bloody Mama (1970) 51; 221; E14.

Blue Dahlia (George Marshall 1946) 23, 120; 43.

Blue Lamp (1950) 62; 215.

Blue White and Perfect (Herbert I. Leeds 1941) 152.

Body and Soul (1947) 173; 48, 87, 160; *3*.

Bodyguard (1948) 77.

Bonnie and Clyde (Arthur Penn 1967) *95*; E15.

Bonnie Parker Story (William Witney 1958) E15.

Boomerang! (Elia Kazan 1947) 5, 20, 46, 117.

Border G-Man (David Howard 1938) E90.

Border Incident (1949) 137; 142.

Borderline (William Seiter 1950) 4, 37, 209.

Born Reckless (1930) 82.

Borsalino (Jacques Deray 1970) 22, 64.

Boss (Byron Haskin 1956) 158.

Boston Blackie and the Law (D. Ross Lederman 1946) 148.

Boston Blackie Booked on Suspicion (Arthur Dreifuss 1945) 148.

Boston Blackie's Chinese Venture (Seymour Friedman 1949) 148.

Boston Blackie Goes Hollywood (Michael Gordon 1942) 148.

Boston Blackie's Rendezvous (Arthur Dreifuss 1945) 148.

Boston Strangler (1969) 77.

Bowery (1933) 213.

Bowery Boy (William Morgan 1940) 84.

Boy of the Streets (William Nigh 1937) 35.

Boys of the City (1940) 129.

Brain *see Le Cerveau.*

Brasher Doubloon/High Window (John Brahm 1947) 43.

Brass Knuckles (1927) 11.

Breathless *see A Bout de Souffle.*

Bribe (Robert Z. Leonard 1949) 201; 175.

Brighton Rock (John Boulting 1947) 9.

Broadway (William Seiter 1942) 53, 168.

Broadway Bad (Sidney Lanfield 1933) 27, 52.

Brotherhood (Martin Ritt 1968) 2, 45; E136.

Brother Orchid (1941) 11; 21, 28, 112, 171; 103.

Brothers Rico (1957) 115; 49; *95.*

Brute Force (1947) 59; 26, 122, 202; *175;* 103; E164.

Build My Gallows High *see* Out of the Past.

Bulldog Drummond in Africa (Louis King 1938) 151, 167.

Bulldog Drummond's Bride (James Hogan 1939) 45.

Bulldog Drummond Strikes Back (1934) 65.

Bullet for Joey (Lewis Allen 1955) 168, 171, 205; 25.

Bullet Is Waiting (1954) 75.

Bullets for O'Hara (William K. Howard 1941) 167.

Bullets or Ballots (1936) 116; 27, 28, 134, 171.

Bullitt (1969) 224; 119.

Bunco Squad (Herbert I. Leeds 1950) 52.

Bureau of Missing Persons (1933) 65; 60,

Gary Cooper (left), Guy Kibbee (right) in CITY STREETS

74, 112, 196.

Burglar (Paul Wendkos 1957) 72; 92.

Busy Body (William Castle 1967) 177, 142.

Butch Minds the Baby (Alfred S. Rogell 1942) 26, 53, 176.

Buy Me That Town (Eugene Forde 1941) 126, 152.

C

Caged (1950) 56; 191; *190*; E164.

Cage of Gold (1950) 62; 130.

Calling Homicide (Edward Bernds 1956) 198.

Call Northside 777 (1948) 98; 46, 49, 187, 194.

Canary Murder Case (Mal St. Clair 1929) 7, 163.

Cape Fear (J. Lee Thompson 1961) 146.

Captive City (1952) 222; 202; *89*.

Car 99 (Charles Barton 1935) 179.

Casbah (John Berry 1948) 131.

Case against Brooklyn (Paul Wendkos 1958) 145.

Case of the Curious Bride (1935) 57; 112, 134, 219.

Case of the Howling Dog (Alan Crosland 1934) 8, 112, 219.

Case of the Lucky Legs (1936) 140; 112, 134, 198, 219.

Castle on the Hudson (Anatole Litvak 1940) 87, 155.

Cave se rebiffe (Gilles Grangier 1961) 85.

Cell 2455, Death Row (1955) 180; E164.

Cent Mille Dollars au Soleil/Greed In the Sun (Henry Verneuil 1963) 22, 211.

Cerveau/Brain (Gérard Oury 1969) 22.

Chain Gang (1950) 123.

Chance Meeting *see* Blind Date.

Charlie Chan at the Wax Museum (Lynn Shores 1940) 125.

Chase (Arthur Ripley 1946) 47, 131; 223, 225.

Chicago (Frank Urson 1928) 52.

Chicago Calling (John Reinhardt 1952) 72.

Chicago Confidential (Sidney Salkow 1957) 50, 88, 121.

Chicago Deadline (Lewis Allen 1949) 88, 117, 120; *182*.

Chicago Syndicate (1955) 180; 195.

Circumstantial Evidence (Charles La-mont 1935) 202.

City Is Dark/Crime Wave (Andre de Toth 1954) 32, 42, 63, 100.

City of Chance (1940) 52.

City of Fear (1959) 127; 198.

City Streets (Rouben Mamoulian 1931) 183; *89*; 96.

Clan des Siciliens (Henri Verneuil 1969) 64, 85; E136.

City That Never Sleeps (John H. Auer 1953) 6, 199.

Classe Tous Risques/Big Risk (Claude Sautet 1959) 22, 211.

Cloportes (Pierre Granier-Deferre 1966) 211.

Close Call for Boston Blackie (1946) 123.

Code of the Streets (1938) 75.

Code Two (Fred M. Wilcox 1953) 143.

Colonel March Investigates (Cyril End-field 1953) 114.

Colour Me Dead (Eddie Davis 1968) 113.

Come On (Russell Birdwell 1956) 100.

Concrete Jungle *see* The Criminal.

Condemned Women (1938) 123.

Confessions of Boston Blackie (1942) 69.

Convicted (Henry Levin 1950) 20, 53, 81; *95*; 223.

Convicted Woman (1940) 94; 81.

Convicts Four (Millard Kaufman 1962) 42, 53.

Coogan's Bluff (1969) 184; 46.

James Shigata in Fuller's THE CRIMSON KIMONO

Frank Sinatra arrives on the scene as THE DETECTIVE

Désordre et la Nuit (Gilles Grangier 1958) 85.

Desperate (1947) 137; 37.

Desperate Cargo (1941) 17.

Desperate Hours (William Wyler 1955) 28, 88, 117, 202; *89.*

Detective (1969) 71; 135, 143, 185.

Detective Story (William Wyler 1951) 23, 135; *89; 225.*

Deuxième Souffle (1966) 144; 211.

Devil Is a Sissy (1936) 35/210; 172.

Dick Tracy (William Berke 1946) *216.*

Dick Tracy Meets Gruesome (John Rawlins 1947) 114.

Dick Tracy's Dilemma (John Rawlins 1947) 121.

Dillinger (Max Nosseck 1945) 45, 50, 125; 225; E68.

Disorderly Conduct (John Considine 1932) 21, 208.

D.O.A. (Rudolph Maté 1949) 2, 30, 88, 154; 174.

Docks of New York (1928) 212; 13.

Don't Turn 'Em Loose (Benjamin Stoloff 1936) 196.

Doomed To Die (William Nigh 1940) 114.

Doorway to Hell (1930) 140; 38; 35.

Doulos/Finger Man (1962) 144; 22.

Down Three Dark Streets (Arnold Laven 1954) 1, 53.

Dragnet (1928) 212; 13, 163.

Dragon Murder Case (H. Bruce Humbertstone 1935) 198, 219.

Dressed To Kill (Eugene Forde 1941) 152.

Drive a Crooked Road (Richard Quine 1954) 172.

Dual Alibi (Alfred Travers 1947) 130.

Duffy of San Quentin (Walter Doninger 1954) 135.

Du Rififi Chez les Femmes/Rififi and the Women (Alex Joffé 1958) 105.

Du Rififi Chez les Hommes/Rififi (1954) 59; 105.

Dust Be My Destiny (1939) 181; 87, 125, 155; 173.

E

Each Dawn I Die (1939) 116; 13, 38, 168.

Earl of Chicago (Richard Thorpe 1940) 6, 147.

East of the River (Alfred E. Green 1940) 87

Edge of Eternity (1959) 184; *95.*

Ellery Queen and the Murder Ring (James Hogan 1941) 21.

Ellery Queen and the Perfect Crime (James Hogan 1941) 21.

Ellery Queen, Master Detective (Kurt Neumann 1940) 21.

Ellery Queen's Penthouse Mystery (James Hogan 1941) 21, 45.

Emergency Squad (1939) 69; 167.

The Enforcer/Murder Incorporated

(1951) 213; 28, 63, 121; E150.

Ernest Hemingway's The Killers *see* Killers (1954)

Escape from San Quentin (1957) 180; E164.

Escape in the Desert (Edward A. Blatt 1945) 140.

Etoile de Valencia (Alfred Zeisler and Serge de Poligny 1933) 85.

Ex Mrs. Bradford (Stephen Roberts 1936) 7.

Experiment Alcatraz (1950) 147.

Eyes in the Night (Fred Zinnemann 1942) 6, 12.

Eyes of the Underworld (Roy William Neill 1942) 21, 125, 219.

Aftermath of violence in PAY OR DIE

F

Falcon in Danger (William Clemens 1943) *216*.

Falcon in Hollywood (1944) 71, 126.

Falcon in San Francisco (1945) 129.

Falcon Out West (William Clemens 1944) 198.

Falcon's Alibi (William Berke 1946) 50.

Falcon's Brother (Stanley Logan 1942) *216*; E165.

Falcon Strikes Back (1943) 69; *216*

Falcon Takes Over (Irving Reis 1942) 43.

Fallen Angel (Otto Preminger 1945) 5, 26; 119.

Fall Guy (Reginald Le Borg 1947) 50; 223.

False Faces/Let 'Em Have It (Sam Wood 1935) E68.

Farewell My Lovely *see* Murder My Sweet.

Fatal Hour (William Nigh 1940) 114.

F.B.I. Code 98 (Leslie H. Martinson 1962) 58.

F.B.I. Girl (William Berke 1951) 37, 205; E76.

F.B.I. Story (1959) 128; 194; *190*; E76.

Feathered Serpent (1949) 17.

Federal Fugitives (1941) 17.

Federal Man (Robert Tansey 1950) 198.

Federal Manhunt (1938) 94; 84.

Félins/Love Cage/Joy House (René Clément 1964) 64.

Female on the Beach (1955) 160; 191.

Fiend Who Walked the West (1958) 71; 145; 101, 225.

File on Thelma Jordan (1949) 186; 188.

Finger Man *see Doulos*.

Finger Points (John Francis Dillon 1931) 86; 36.

Fingerprints (1926) 11.

Five against the House (1955) 115; 48, 153.

Five Steps to Danger (Henry S. Kesler 1957) 100.

Floods of Fear (1958) 54.

Fog Over 'Frisco (1934) 67; 60, 198.

Follow Me Quietly (1949) 77.

Force of Evil (Abraham Polonsky 1949) 91, 126; *3, 169*.

Forgotten Faces (Victor Schertzinger 1927) 33.

For the Defence (1930) 56.

Framed (Richard Wallace 1947) 81, 197.

Free Soul (Clarence Brown 1931) 86.

Frightened City *see* Killer That Stalked New York.

Frisco Kid (1935) 11; 134.

From Headquarters (1933) 67.

Front Page Woman (1936) 57; 151.

Full Confession (1939) 75; 40; *216*.

Full Sun *see Plein Soleil*.

G

Gambling House (1950) 203; 23, 139; *216*.

Gang Buster (A. Edward Sutherland 1931) 7.

Gangs of Chicago (Arthur Lubin 1940) 134, 152.

Gangs of New York (James Cruze 1938) 26, 84.

Frank Sinatra in A HOLE IN THE HEAD

H

Robert Taylor with Audrey Totter in HIGH WALL

Hell Drivers (Cy Endfield 1958) 12, 130.
Hell Is a City (Val Guest 1959) 12.
Hell on 'Frisco Bay (Frank Tuttle 1955) 120, 171, 195; *182, 190.*
Hell's Highway (1932) 35.
Hell's House (Howard Higgins 1932) 60, 155.
Hell's Kitchen (1939) 181; 61.
He Ran All the Way (John Berry 1951) 87, 221; *107.*
He Walked by Night (Alfred Werker 1948) 137.
Hidden Eye (Richard Whorf 1945) 6.
Hidden Fear (Andre de Toth 1957) 158.
Hideout (1934) 210; 6.
High Pressure (1932) 128; 163.
High School Confidential (Jack Arnold 1958) 191, 198.
High Sierra (1941) 213; 28, 117, 133; 103, 110; 36; E68.
High Wall (Curtis Bernhardt 1948) 4, 201, 205.
Highway Dragnet (Nathan Juran 1954) 49; 51.
Highway 301 (Andrew Stone 1950) 47, 73.
Highway West (William McGann 1941) 117.
High Window *see* Brasher Doubloon.
His Kind of Woman (1951) 75; 37, 142, 146; 108.
Hitch-Hiker (1953) 133, 154, 199.
Hold Your Man (Sam Wood 1933) 97.
Hole *see Trou.*
Hole in the Wall (1929) 79; 171.

Homicide Bureau (C. C. Coleman 1938) 125.
Homicide Squad (1931) 39; 151.
Hoodlum Empire (Joseph Kane 1952) 2, 70, 209.
Hoodlum Saint (Norman Taurog 1946) 163, 196.
Hot Car Girl (Bernard Kowalski 1958) 121; 51.
Hot Rod Gang (1958) 123.
Hot Spot/ I Wake Up Screaming (Bruce Humberstone 1941) 4, 50, 139.
The House across the Bay (1940) 140; 152, 168.
House Is Not a Home (1964) 174; 53, 201, 221.
House of Bamboo (1955) 84; 66, 177; 119.
House of Numbers (1957) 174; 42, 156; E164.
House of the Seven Hawks (Richard Thorpe 1959) 201.
House of Women (Walter Doniger 1962) E164.
House on 92nd Street (1946) 98; 152; E76.
Houston Story (William Castle 1956) 6.
How To Murder a Rich Uncle (1957) 157.
Human Cargo (Allan Dwan 1956) 70, 209.
Human Jungle (Joe Newman 1954) 145, 191.
Hunted Men (Louis King 1938) 167.
Hush Money (Sidney Lanfield 1931) 132, 168.

Susan Hayward as the condemned woman in I WANT TO LIVE

I

I Am a Fugitive from a Chain Gang (1932) 128; 6, 74, 83, 112, 149; *161*.

I Am a Thief (1935) 79; 8.

I Am the Law (Alexander Hall 1938) 125, 171.

I Died a Thousand Times (1955) 101; 138, 156, 221; 36; E68.

Illegal (Lewis Allen 1955) 1, 171; *190*; 36.

I'll Get You for This *see* Lucky Nick Cain.

Illicit (1931) 140; 21, 27, 52, 188.

I Loved a Woman (Alfred E. Green 1933) 171.

I Love Trouble (S. Sylvan Simon 1947) 45, 74.

I Mobster (1958) 51; 47.

In Cold Blood (1967) 34; 142, 195.

Informers (Ken Annakin 1963) 157.

Innocents of Chicago (Lupino Lane 1931) E44.

Inside Detroit (1956) 180; 155.

Inside Job (Jean Yarborough 1946) 83.

Inside the Mafia (1959) 39; 63; E136.

Inside the Walls of Folsom Prison (Crane Wilbur 1951) 31, 47, 63.

Interpol (John Gilling 1956) 106, 139.

In the Nick (1959) 109.

Intrigue (Edward L. Marin 1947) 168.

Invisible Stripes (1939) 11; 28, 125, 168.

I Stole a Million (Frank Tuttle 1939) 168, 209.

It All Came True (1940) 181; 28; 103.

It Had to Happen (1936) 65; 168.

I the Jury (Harry Essex, 1953) 50, 83.

It Takes All Kinds (Eddie Davis 1968) 197.

I Wake Up Screaming *see* Hot Spot.

I Walk Alone (Byron Haskin 1947) 122, 125, 141.

I Want To Live (1958) 222; 214; E164.

I Was a Convict (Aubrey Scotto 1939) 134.

J

Jack of Diamonds (Vernon Sewell 1949) 157.

Jailbreak (1936) 94; 134.

Jail Busters (1955) 17; 134.

Jailhouse Blues (Albert S. Rogell 1941) 135.

Jeu de la Verité (1961) 105.

Je Vous Salue Mafia (Raoul Levy 1966) E136.

Jewel Robbery (1932) 67; 163.

Jigsaw (Fletcher Markle 1949) 215.

Jimmy the Gent (1934) 57; 60, 112.

Joe Macbeth (1955) 109; 225.

Johnny Allegro (1949) 203; 168.

Johnny Angel (Edward L. Marin 1945) 168, 209.

Johnny Apollo (1940) 98; 6, 125, 152.

Johnny Cool (William Asher 1963) 40, 50, 125; E136.

Johnny Eager (1941) 128; 6, 74, 195, 201.

Johnny O'Clock (1947) 173; 46, 162; *95*.

Johnny One Eye (1949) 79; 155; 176.

Johnny Stool Pigeon (William Castle 1949) 72, 221.

Joker Is Wild (Charles Vidor 1957) 63, 88, 185.

Charles McGraw with Harry Hayden and
William Conrad in Siodmak's version of THE KILLERS

Journal of a Crime (1934) 116.
Joy House *see Félins*
Juke Girl (Curtis Bernhardt 1942) 25.
Junior G-Men (Ford Beebe, John

Rawlins 1940) E90.
Junior G-Men of the Air (Ray Taylor, Lewis D. Collins 1942) E90.

K

Kansas City Confidential (1952) 115; 30, 83, 158; 35.
The Kennel Murder Case (1933) 57; 8, 163.
Key Largo (1948) 110; 10, 28, 91, 125, 171, 209; 34.
Kid Galahad (1937) 57; 28, 60.
Kid Galahad (1962) 115; 32.
Killer at Large (1947) 17.
Killer Dill (Lewis D. Collins 1947) 141.
Killers (1946) 186; 48, 121, 122, 142, 154; *175*; 103.
Killers/Ernest Hemingway's The Killers (1964) 184; 138.
Killer That Stalked New York/Frightened City (Earl McEvoy 1950) 73.
Killing (Stanley Kubrick 1956) 1, 42, 50,

63, 100, 179.
King of Alcatraz (1938) 79; 167, 200.
King of Chinatown (1939) 94; 167, 200.
King of Gamblers (1937) 79; 152, 200, 209.
King of the Underworld (1939) 181; 28, 36.
Kiss Me Deadly (1955) 3; 121, 143, 195; 25.
Kiss of Death (1947) 98; 70, 139, 218; 101.
Kiss the Blood off My Hands (Norman Foster 1948) 122; *175*.
Kiss Tomorrow Goodbye (1950) 71; 2, 38, 134.
Knock on Any Door (1949) 170; 28; *95*.

L

Ladies Love Brutes (Rowland V. Lee 1930) 8, 13.
Ladies of the Big House (Marion Gering 1932) 183; E164.
Ladies of the Mob (1928) 217.
Lady and the Mob (Ben Stoloff 1939) 133, 179.
Lady for a Day (Frank Capra 1933) 74; 176.
Lady Gangster (1942) 79; 135.
Lady in Cement (1968) 71; 49, 185.

Lady in the Death House (Steve Sekely 1942) E164.
Lady in the Lake (1947) 147; 4, 147, 152, 205; 43.
Lady in the Morgue (Otis Garrett 1938) 83.
Lady Killer (1933) 65.
Ladykillers (Alexander Mackendrick 1956) 130, 215.
Lady Scarface (Frank Woodruff 1941) 125, 135; E41.

James Cagney with Doris Day in LOVE ME OR LEAVE ME

Lady without a Passport (1950) 129; *169*.
Larceny (George Sherman 1948) 72, 158, 221.
Larceny Inc. (1942) 11; 53, 167, 171.
Last Gangster (Edward Ludwig 1937) 171, 187, 194; 217.
Last Gangster *see* Roger Touhy Gangster.
Last Mile (Sam Bischoff 1932) 83; E164.
Last Mile (Howard W. Koch 1959) 172; E164.
Last Warning (Albert S. Rogell 1938) 83.
Las Vegas Shakedown (Sidney Salkow 1955) 91.
Las Vegas Story (Robert Stevenson 1952) 66, 139.
Lavender Hill Mob (1951) 54.
Law and Disorder (1958) 54.
Law of the Underworld (1938) 123; 45, 148.
Law vs. Gangsters (Leslie Martinson 1958) E213.
Lawyer Man (1932) 67; 27, 112, 163.
League of Frightened Men (Alfred E. Green 1937) 6, 45, 187.
League of Gentlemen (1960) 62; 9, 157.
Lemon Drop Kid (Marshall Neilan 1934) 176.
Lemon Drop Kid (Sidney Lanfield 1951) 152, 176.
Let 'Em Have It *see* False Faces.
Let No Man Write My Epitaph (Philip Leacock 1959) 221; *95*.
Life in the Balance (Harry Horner 1954) 138.
Line-Up (1958) 184; 145.
Little Big Shot (1935) 57; 74.

Little Caesar (1931) 128; 74, 171; 36.
Little Giant (1933) 65; 8, 171.
Little Miss Marker (Alexander Hall 1934) 26, 53, 176.
Little Red Monkey (1954) 109; 49.
Loi des Rues (Ralph Habib 1956) 211.
Loan Shark (Seymour Friedman 1952) 168, 195.
Locked Door (George Fitzmaurice 1929) 188.
Lone Wolf Keeps a Date (Sidney Salkow 1940) 219.
Lone Wolf Meets a Lady (Sidney Salkow 1940) 219.
Lone Wolf Spy Hunt (Peter Godfrey 1939) 133, 219.
Lone Wolf Strikes (Sidney Salkow 1940) 219.
Lone Wolf Takes a Chance (Sidney Salkow 1941) 219.
Long Haul (1957) 109; 139.
Long Wait (Victor Saville 1954) 1, 167.
Looking for Trouble (Philip Grosset 1953) 179.
Loophole (Harold Schuster 1954) 142, 197.
Lost Lady (Alfred E. Green 1934) 198.
Love Cage *see Félins*.
Love Me Or Leave Me (Charles Vidor 1955) 38.
Lucky Jordan (Frank Tuttle 1943) 120, 126; *182*.
Lucky Nick Cain/I'll Get You for This (Joseph Newman 1951) 168.
Lucky Stiff (Lewis Foster 1949) 70, 209; 179.
Lured (Douglas Sirk 1947) 40, 114.

Jean Gabin in MAIGRET SETS A TRAP

M

M (1931) 124; 131.

M (Joseph Losey 1951) 2, 37; *3*.

Macao (1952) 212; 23, 66, 91, 93, 146; 108.

Machine Gun Kelly (1958) 51; 32, 121.

Madame Racketeer (Alexander Hall, Harry Gribble 1932) 168.

Mad Game (Irving Cummings 1933) 151, 208, 209.

Madigan (1968) 184; 218.

Mafia (Pietro Germi 1949) E136.

Mafioso (Alberto Lattuada 1962) E136.

Magnet of Doom *see Aîné des Ferchaux.*

Maigret et l'Affair Saint Fiacre (Jean Delannoy 1958) 85.

Maigret Sets a Trap *see Maigret Tend un Piège.*

Maigret Tend un Piège/Maigret Sets a Trap (Jean Delannoy 1959) 85, 211.

Main Street after Dark (1944) 39; 72, 205.

Maltese Falcon/Dangerous Female (1931) 65; 52, 96.

Maltese Falcon (1941) 110; 8, 28, 50, 131, 134; 96.

Man Crazy (1954) 127; 30, 225.

Man from Chicago (Walter Summers 1931) E44.

Manhandled (Lewis Foster 1949) 72, 100.

Manhattan Melodrama (1934) 210; 86, 132, 163, 172; *107*; E68.

Man Inside (John Gilling 1958) 156, 157.

Man in the Dark (1953) 123; 63, 135, 154, 205.

Man Is Armed (Franklin Adreon 1956) 134, 199.

Man Named Rocca *see Nomme la Rocca.*

Man on the Prowl (Art Napoleon 1957) 63.

Man Wanted (1932) 67.

Man Who Cheated Himself (Felix Feist 1950) 46.

Man with the Golden Arm (Otto Preminger 1955) 145, 153, 185.

Marked Woman (1937) 11; 28, 45, 60, 112; 173; E150.

Marlowe (Paul Bogart 1969) 43.

Mary Burns Fugitive (William K. Howard 1937) 183, 214.

Mayor of Hell (1933) 140; 38, 112; E164.

Meet Boston Blackie (1941) 79; 148.

Meet Danny Wilson (1951) 160; 37, 185, 221.

Meet Nero Wolfe (Herbert Biberman 1936) 6, 187.

Mefiez Vous Fillettes (Yves Allegret 1957) 105.

Me Gangster (1928) 213.

Melodie en Sous Sol/Big Snatch (Henri Verneuil 1962) 64, 85.

Men of San Quentin (1942) 17.

Meurtrier (Claude Autant-Lara 1962) 105.

Miami Exposé (1956) 180; 6, 46.

Miami Story (1954) 180; 2, 50, 88, 197.

Michael Shayne Private Detective (Eugene Forde 1941) 152.

Midnight (Chester Erskine 1934) 28.

Midnight Club (Alexander Hall 1933) 168.

Midnight Story/Appointment with a Shadow (1958) 160; 63.

Midnight Taxi (John Adolfi 1928) 70, 132; E166.

Mighty (1929) 56; 13.

Millerson Case (George Archainbaud 1947) 16.

Millionaire (John Adolfi 1931) 38.

Million Dollar Ransom (Murray Roth 1934) 6; 176.

James Cagney (seated) with Royal Dano, Robert
Wilke, Sanford Seegar, Bill Green and Herbie Faye
in NEVER STEAL ANYTHING SMALL

Miracle Man (Norman Z. McLeod 1932) 114, 148, 183.
Miroir (Raymond Lamy 1947) 85.
Miss Pinkerton (1932) 11; 27.
Mister Ace (Edward L. Marin 1946) 168, 183.
Mister Cory (Blake Edwards 1957) 26.
Mister District Attorney (William Morgan 1941) 131.
Mister 880 (Edmund Goulding 1950) 122.
Mister Lucky (H. C. Potter 1943) 26, 195; *216.*
Mr. Moto on Danger Island (Herbert I. Leeds 1939) 131.
Mr Moto's Gamble (James Tinling 1938) 131.
Mr. Moto's Last Warning (Norman Foster 1938) 52, 131; *169.*
Mr. Moto Takes a Chance (Norman Foster 1938) 131.
Mr. Moto Takes a Vacation (Norman Foster 1939) 131.
Mr. Wong Detective (William Nigh 1938) 114.
Mr. Wong in Chinatown (William Nigh 1939) 114.
Mob (Robert Parrish 1951) 1, 29, 30, 53, 118, 145.
Moment of Danger (1960) 24; 106.
Money Trap (Burt Kennedy 1966) 81.
Mouthpiece (James Flood, Elliott Nugent 1932) 151, 219.

Moving Finger (Larry Moyer 1963) 187.
Moving Target *see* Harper
Murder by Contract (1958) 127.
Murder Incorporated (1951) *see* Enforcer.
Murder Incorporated (Burt Balaban, Stuart Rosenberg 1961) E150.
Murder in Times Square (1943) 123.
Murder Man (Tim Whelan 1935) 194.
Murder My Sweet/Farewell My Lovely (1945) 69, 141, 162, 209; 43.
Murder of Doctor Harrigan (Frank MacDonald 1935) 8.
Murder with Pictures (Charles Barton 1936) *203.*
Muss 'Em Up (Charles Vidor 1936) 83.
Mutiny in the Big House (William Nigh 1939) 26, 134; E164.
My Brother's Keeper (Alfred Roome 1949) 215.
My Name Is Julia Ross (1945) 129.
My Six Convicts (Hugo Fregonese 1952) 1, 32; E164.
My Son Is Guilty (Charles Barton 1939) 81.
Mysterious Intruder (William Castle 1946) 141.
Mystery in Mexico (1948) 222; 52.
Mystery of Mr. Wong (William Nigh 1939) 114.
Mystery Street (John Sturges 1950) 191; 34.
My True Story (1951) 172.

N

Naked Alibi (Jerry Hopper 1954) 93, 100.
Naked City (1948) 59; 63; *175;* 103.
Naked Street (Maxwell Shane 1955) 167.
Narrow Margin (1952) 77; 142.
Never Love a Stranger (1958) 193; *89.*

Never Steal Anything Small (Charles Lederer 1959) 38, 135, 159.
New Face in Hell *see* P.J.
New Orleans Uncensored/Riot on Pier 6 (William Castle 1955) 88, 141.

Marlon Brando with
Eva Marie Saint in ON THE WATERFRONT

New York Confidential (1955) 174; 49, 53, 141, 151; E150.

Nice Little Bank That Should Be Robbed (Henry Levin 1958) 172.

Nick Carter Master Detective (1939) 207.

Night after Night (1932) 140, 168.

Night and the City (1950) 59; 130, 141, 218.

Night Court (1932) 210; 103.

Nightfall (1956) 207; 92; *95*.

Night for Crime (Alex Thurn-Taxis 1942) 74, 198.

Night in New Orleans (William Clemens 1942) 83.

Night Ride (John S. Robertson 1930) 171.

Night World (Hobart Henley 1932) 168.

99 River Street (1954) 115; 1, 66, 121, 158.

Nocturne (Edward L. Marin 1947) 168; 35.

Nomme La Rocca/Man Named Rocca (Jean Becker 1961) 22.

Noose (Edmond T. Greville 1948) 40, 157.

Noose Hangs High (Charles Barton 1948) 40, 141.

No Questions Asked (Harold K. Kress 1951) 197.

No Trees in the Street (J. Lee Thompson 1958) 130.

No Way Out (Joseph L. Mankiewicz 1950) 218.

Numbered Men (1930) 128.

O

Ocean's 11 (Lewis Milestone 1960) 49, 185, 200.

Odds against Tomorrow (1959) 222; 20, 93, 177, 221.

Once a Thief (Ralph Nelson 1965) 64, 156.

On Dangerous Ground (1951) 170; 20, 133, 177; 25.

One Body Too Many (Frank Mac-Donald 1944) 198.

One Way Street (Hugo Fregonese 1950) 48, 72.

On Friday at Eleven (Alvin Rakoff 1960) 189.

Only When I Larf (1968) 62; 9.

On the Waterfront (Elia Kazan 1954) 46, 159, 189.

Out of the Fog (Anatole Litvak 1941) 87 133, 173.

Out of the Past/Build My Gallows High (1947) 207; 78, 146; *216*.

Outside the Law (Jack Arnold 1956) 58, 171.

Outside the Wall (Crane Wilbur 1950) 160.

Jack Webb with
Janet Leigh in PETE KELLY'S BLUES

Pacha (George Lautner 1968) 85.

Panic in the Streets (Elia Kazan 1950) 145, 156, 218.

Parachute Jumper (Alfred E. Green 1933) 60.

Parole (1936) 123; 167.

Parole Fixer (1940) 79; 167, 198.

Parole Girl (Edward F. Cline 1933) 21.

Party Girl (1958) 170; 46, 52, 201.

Passport to Shame (Alvin Rakoff 1958) 130.

Pay or Die (Richard Wilson 1960) 29; *169*; E136.

Penalty (Wallace Worsley 1920) 33.

Penalty (Harold S. Bucquet 1941) 6.

Pendulum (George Schaefer 1968) 118, 142.

Pépé le Moko (Julien Duvivier 1937) 85.

Pépé le Moko (Julien Duvivier 1951) 85.

Persons in Hiding (Louis King 1939) 151; E15.

Pete Kelly's Blues (Jack Webb 1955) 138, 154.

Petrified Forest (1936) 140; 28, 60 179; *161*.

Phantom Killer (1942) 17.

Phantom Raiders (1939) 207.

Phenix City Story (1955) 115; 118.

Pick-Up (Marion Gering 1933) 168, 183.

Pick-Up on South Street (1953) 84; 118, 218.

Picture Snatcher (1933) 11; 21.

P.J./New Face in Hell (John Guillermin 1967) 37; E165.

Platinum High School/Rich Young and Deadly (Charles Haas 1960) 50, 72, 172.

Plein Soleil/Full Sun/Purple Noon (René Clément 1959) 64.

Plunder of the Sun (1953) 75; 81.

Plunder Road (Hubert Cornfield 1957) 50.

Pocketful of Miracles (Frank Capra 1961) 31, 60, 126, 141; 176.

Point Blank (John Boorman 1967) 138; E164.

Port of New York (1949) 24.

Portrait of a Mobster (1961) 160; 58; *190*.

Power of the Whistler (1945) 123.

Pretty Boy Floyd (Herbert J. Leder 1959) E80.

Prison Break (Arthur Rubin 1938) 74, 134; E164.

Prison Farm (Louis King 1938) 151.

Prison des Femmes (Maurice Cloché 1962) E164.

Prison Warden (Seymour Friedman 1949) 16.

Prison without Bars (Brian Desmond Hurst 1938) E164.

Prize of Arms (Cliff Owen 1961) 12.

Prize of Gold (Mark Robson 1954) 157, 218.

Private Detective 62 (1933) 57; 163.

Private Hell 36 (1954) 184; 47, 133; *95*.

Prowl Car *see* Between Midnight and Dawn.

Prowler (Joseph Losey 1951) *3*.

Public Defender (J. Walter Rubin 1931) 114.

Public Enemy (1931) 217; 27, 38, 97; E44.

Public Enemy's Wife/G-Man's Wife (1936) 94; 155.

Public Enemies (Albert S. Rogell 1941) 125.

Public Hero No. 1 (J. Walter Rubin 1935) 7, 40, 148; E68.

Wanda Hendrix and Robert
Montgomery in RIDE A PINK HORSE

Purple Gang (Frank MacDonald 1959) 197.

Purple Noon *see Plein Soleil*.
Pushover (Richard Quine 1954) 153.

Q

Quai des Blondes (Paul Cadeo 1953) 105.
Queen of the Mob (James Hogan 1940) 21, 151, 177; E14.

Quick Millions (1931) 35; 168, 208.
Quicksand (Irving Pichel 1950) 131, 172.

R

Race Street (Edward L. Marin 1948) 23, 168.
Racket (Lewis Milestone 1928) 108.
Racket (1951) 56; 48, 146, 177, 199; 36, 108.
Racket Busters (1938) 11; 28, 112; 173.
Racketeers in Exile (Erle C. Kenton 1937) 13.
Racket Man (D. Ross Lederman 1944) 221.
Radio Patrol (1932) 39.
Railroaded (1947) 137.
Raw Deal (1948) 137; 37.
Razzia sur la Chnouf (Henri Decoin 1955) 85, 211.
Red Hot and Blue (1949) 75; 139.
Red Light (1949) 65; 37, 134, 168.
Remember That Face (Robert Parrish 1952) 1, 29, 30, 53, 118, 145.
Revenue Agent (1950) 123; 198; E204.
Revolt in the Big House (R. G. Springsteen 1958) 42, 145.
Rich Young and Deadly *see* Platinum High School.
Ride a Crooked Mile (Alfred E. Green 1938) 200; E164.
Ride the Pink Horse (1947) 147; 91; 101.
Rififi *see Du Rififi Chez les Hommes*.

Rififi and the Women *see Du Rififi Chez les Femmes*.
Rififi in Tokyo (Jacques Deray 1964) E59.
Riley the Cop (1928) 82; E166.
Riot (Buzz Kulik 1968) E164.
Riot in Juvenile Prison (1959) 39.
Riot in Cell Block 11 (1954) 184; 30, 145; 214; E164.
Riot on Pier 6 *see* New Orleans Uncensored.
Rise and Fall of Legs Diamond (Budd Boetticher 1959) 58.
Road Block (Harold Daniels 1951) 142.
Road House (Jean Negulesco 1948) 133, 218.
Road to Alcatraz (1945) 94.
Roaring Twenties (1939) 213; 28, 38, 179; 103, 173; E166.
Robbery (1967) 224; 12.
Robin and the Seven Hoods (1964) 71; 112, 171, 185.
Rock All Night (1957) 51.
Roger Touhy Gangster/Last Gangster (1944) 79; 83, 167; E206.
Rogue Cop (Roy Rowland 1954) 168, 201; *182*.

Farley Granger (left) in SIDE STREET

Cary Grant (left) in MR. LUCKY

T

Dolores Dorn with
Cliff Robertson in UNDERWORLD U.S.A.

U

V

Vacanze Col Gangster (Dino Risi 1951) 125.
Very Honorable Guy (1934) 11; 176.
Vice Squad (1931) 56; 171, 220.
Vice Squad (Arnold Laven 1953) 1, 171, 220.
Vicious Years (1950) 79.
Violent Playground (1958) 62; 12.
Violent Saturday (1955) 77; 29, 66, 73, 138, 139, 151, 183.

W

Warning Shot (Buzz Kulik 1967) 20.
Waterfront at Midnight (William Berke 1948) 135.
Way to the Gold (Robert D. Webb 1957) 30, 197.
We're No Angels (1954) 57; 28.
West Side Story (1961) 222.
Wet Parade (Victor Fleming 1932) 111, 132, 196; E166.
Wharf Angel (William Cameron Menzies 1934) 83, 179.
When Gangland Strikes (R. G. Springsteen 1956) 4.
When G-Men Step In (C. C. Coleman 1938) 135; E90.
Where the Sidewalk Ends (Otto Preminger 1950) 5, 30; 101.
While the City Sleeps (1956) 124; 5, 78, 133.
Whipsaw (Sam Wood 1935) 132, 208; 107.
Whistling in the Dark/Scared (Elliott Nugent 1933) 6.
White Heat (1949) 213; 38, 47, 154; 190; E204.
Whole Town's Talking (1935) 82; 7, 171; 36.
Wide Boy (1952) 109.
Widow from Chicago (Edward Cline 1930) 171; E44.
Wife Wanted (1946) 115.
Wild Boys of the Road (1934) 217.
Wild One (1954) 24, 138, 202.
Wild Party (Harry Horner 1956) 159, 195.
Window (1949) 203; 117, 195; 216; 223.
Winterset (Alfred Santell 1936) 45.
Within These Walls (Bruce Humberstone 1945) 192.
Women in Prison (Lambert Hillyer 1937) E164.
Women's Prison (1954) 181; 133, 191, 205; E164.

Y

You and Me (1938) 124; 134, 168, 183.

You Can Never Tell (Lou Breslow 1951) 162; E165.

You Can't Get Away with Murder (19 ?) 181; 28, 179.

Young Dillinger (Terry Morse 1964) 145; E68.

Young Don't Cry (Afred Werker 1957) 151.

Young Man with Ideas (Mitchell Leisen 1952) 126.

Young Savages (John Frankenheimer 1961) 122.

You Only Live Once (1937) 124; 134, 183; 214; E15.